To Dr. Poon.

Leader*shift*

Leaders need 'vision'

thanks for keeping mine healthy

Marcel Latouche

May 14— 2013

Leader*shift*

Collaboration in the 21st Century

Marcel Latouche

Library of Congress Control Number: 2013903287
ISBN: Hardcover   978-1-4797-9827-8
                     Softcover   978-1-4797-9826-1
                     Ebook   978-1-4797-9828-5

This book was printed in the United States of America.

Rev. date: 02/25/2013

To order additional copies of this book, contact:
Xlibris Corporation
1-888-795-4274
www.Xlibris.com
Orders@Xlibris.com
126709

Contents

PART THREE

The Construction

This book is dedicated to my wife Judy for her patience and undivided support

ACKNOWLEDGEMENTS

THIS BOOK IS the culmination of many years of research, and in the broadest sense a collaborative work, because many of the views shared in this book are the result of conversations with many people. After many years of working in large corporations in both the public and private sectors, I have encountered different corporate cultures; as a result I have formed opinions and acquired new beliefs and values. I found writing this book very cathartic and a very revealing experience and thanks to many friends I was able to accomplish this task.

Many people have contributed to make this book possible, and I would like to thank them for their ideas, help, and moral support when it was required. More specifically I would like to thank my former colleagues, my students and Richard Burley for suggesting the title

PREFACE

FOR MANY THE search for happiness is often marked by an emphasis on being more important than the next person. Today we live in a world of confrontation, paranoia, phobia and stress. Our environment is one of an anxiety-driven society, often caused by the search for self-importance. Corporations and other institutions have clued in on that need for importance, and very often they have tailored their policies to match this greed and race for becoming the best. As a result, many employees have been victims of their own traps.

Today, increasingly people are seeking a new lifestyle; one that is often based on happiness not brought about by a continued climb up the corporate ladder, but one more geared to personal satisfaction, sharing and giving of oneself. The hustle and bustle of the past is quickly being changed to a more holistic way of life. More and more people are seeking solace in the practice of meditation, yoga, and the learning of Buddhist and Taoist philosophies. The learning of these philosophies is becoming more prevalent as more people make the distinction between two different cultures: The Western culture mostly based on laws, and the Eastern culture based on relationships.

The idea is that one can learn to control oneself and reach happiness, which can be shared with other people through personal connection. The idea that we can give back to the community and our neighbors is gradually becoming entrenched in our daily lives.

We must stop being adolescents and start behaving like grown ups. We need a *shift* in our leadership beliefs whereby leaders stop doing but, instead, allow people to do.

In the English language the suffix *ship*, has been used to form nouns denoting quality, status, and tenure of office, skill and collective individuals of a group. Added to the word leader, this suffix has often taken a different connotation. Leadership has been associated with good and bad. While many leaders have given much of themselves for the good of their followers, others have misused their status to create chaos to satisfy their greed. In the corporate world of the 90s and in the early days of the new millennium, we have often seen the mistreatment of employees and stakeholders for the sake of the so-called bottom line. Many government leaders have not been better, often using taxpayers' money to further their policies to extend their grip on power. All of this as resulted in many hardships and it is time that we examine another form of leadership.

This is why this book asks for a *shift* in the way that leaders view their mission and why and how they should include more people in the decision-making process. This shift is not only required in corporations, but in governments and unions as well. The collaborative effort requires that all stakeholders be included, because increasingly a leadership vacuum seems to exist. What we need to improve the situation is not only committed and honest leaders, but also a change in ideas, attitude and approach to solving problems. In other words, we need a Leader*shift*.

CHAPTER 1

From Darkness into Light

"Lots of folks confuse bad management with destiny."
                                                    – Kin Hubbard.

IN A NEW millennium, it is astonishing that after all these years the human race still does not seem to be able to learn from its past. While not all the mistakes of the past are repeated, on many occasions we fail to learn from them and continue to use old solutions to solve new problems. To know one's past is a sure way to plan one's future and we should search for parallel events and endeavor to learn, anticipate and adapt.

The events that have occurred in the decades of the 80s and 90s bear some similarity to previous occurrences. In the mid-50s, at least in the United States, for the first time in employment history white-collar workers outnumbered blue-collar workers. This shift in employment demography is one of the many consequences, which ushered in the 'change' movement in management.

Changes in technological developments, globalization, economic and social conditions are but a few factors which affect the very basis of each person's daily routine. Globalization is shrinking the world's boundaries, putting pressure on market share and jobs through increasing competition. Industrialized countries are seeing jobs transferred to developing countries because labor costs there, are in many cases, cheaper. Outsourcing of jobs to developing countries is now a common strategy for many companies. In addition to pressures for better products and services, there is a growing demand for equality, better social and environmental conditions and certainly better rewards for work performed. In the wake of these pressures, organizations are restructuring and reengineering themselves to become more competitive.

At the same time, surveys and studies indicate employees' morale in the industrialized countries is at an all time low. People who once thought they had a secure job quickly found themselves downsized in the latest company restructuring, becoming an addition to the unemployment statistics.

What does this entire means to the average worker? How can we help workers/employees adapt to these changes? Recently, many authors have tried to provide answers to these questions. Each one embraces a different theory, sometimes creating more confusion instead of providing the promised solutions.

This situation is not new. However, there are clear signs that the answer lies in a new form of leadership, which demands a radical **shift** in thinking and implementation. A leadership style, which comes from a bottom/up decision-making structure, one that promotes leaders who are strong and self-confident enough to listen to workers from all levels of the organization – hence the term **Leadershift**. The objective in this work, then, is to look at some values, which we seem to have forgotten, and attempt to bring them back into perspective to facilitate a renewed management style for the next millennium.

In the middle Ages many things were withheld from the masses. Education was reserved for the rich, nobles and a few fortunate others. Mostly the church administered art and literature. The masses worked and existed under a system of fiefdom, governed by nobility and leaders of the church who lived in castles and collected taxes through sheriffs and armies. Then came the Renaissance, which changed many of our concepts about education, art and literature. The resulting freedom of expression of artists, writers and architects has left us with an unprecedented legacy. Innovation and creativity flourished in these times, and civilization moved forward entering a new era of change, growth and prosperity.

Today, the comparison is not much different. Since World War II we have experienced enormous changes in our lives. While we prospered in the 60s and part of the 70s, the explosion in technology accompanied by the effects of globalization has caused the decade spanning the mid-80s and mid-90s, to be one of the darkest eras for management and workers alike. Drastic change is at the heart of our problems and demands that we do things in a different way. We must acquire the flexibility to anticipate, learn and adapt to survive this passing maelstrom.

Unfortunately for us, while events have changed the way we do business, the management of people has not changed significantly. The proliferation of technology and opportunities for higher education has created a new type of worker with more knowledge. However, management in many cases has not recognized this trend and continues to treat employees under the old concepts of management by fear, power and control. Today, many corporations adopt quick fix solutions, which damage rather than improve existing conditions. The result has been a loss of trust and loyalty. In many cases the working environment has been poisoned by poor management decisions, which have left workers, totally demoralized, frustrated, confused, and sometimes mentally abused. As Wright and Smye (1996) indicate:

> "Corporate abuse has the same effect on an organization that pollution has on an ecosystem. It interferes with natural processes. It gums up the works until processes that used to occur spontaneously begin to wither." [1]

Management's lack of understanding that a change in style is necessary has polluted the work environment. In an attempt to remedy the situation, many have tried concepts, which resulted in more damage than repair. It is not that the concepts were totally wrong; poor implementation and excessive rhetoric were mostly the cause of failure. Workers did not know from day to day whether management would adopt a new concept or if other management pronouncements would be upheld. The 'Double-talk' became the norm rather than the exception, in some cases resulting in severe backlashes. For example, while violence on picket lines was once confined to blue-collar workers strikes the new era has brought with it white collar violence. In France, in response to proposed change, Credit Foncier employees kidnapped the bank's president and seven executives and held them hostage, for six days in January of 1997. The hostages were released only after government representatives agreed to negotiations and new alternatives. Is this the type of work environment we have to look forward to?

Then we see corporations' manipulation of the media on issues of great social and health importance. For example, we have seen the way Tobacco Companies have handled their knowledge of the presence of cancer producing chemicals in their products. Or how corporations have handled matters pertaining to environmental accidents, which have damaged coastal economies or destroyed rare environmental habitats.

Governments are no better. Politicians make promises, which are often subsequently broken. Widespread failure to control high levels of deficit spending has led to enormous debt, resulting in economic problems for many industrialized countries. While some have amended their policies, others continue to revel in services and projects financed by increased taxation. As a former civil servant in a large municipality, I have witnessed waste, misinformation by bureaucrats and systematic lack of accountability to the taxpayers. In the absence of proper disclosure, citizens lack the information required to challenge many of the decisions to tax their hard-earned income to finance projects, which promote the agendas of politicians, special interest groups and bureaucrats. The result has been damaging as exemplified by the financial collapse of many European countries. The United States, once the bastion of the free market is teetering on the brink of a 'fiscal cliff', which may or may not be resolved by the time that this book is published.

Events in Canada and other places continue to show governments' attempt to cover-up or camouflage poor decisions. In Canada we can recall The Adscam scandal where the Liberal government was accused of misuse and misdirection of public funds. There also cases where environmental issues have either been ignored or tolerated. In Quebec several Mayors have been accused of fraud and are either under investigation or have been charged. These examples have contributed to the erosion of the public trust in governments, politicians and publicly-owned corporations.

Union leaders pursue the same strategies to try and maintain their past gains. In recent years, competition from developing countries has shifted labor-management dynamics. Unions' no longer command the same bargaining leverage. In the past, unions have relied on solidarity and unity to rally their members. Today, in most large industrialized countries, many unions are losing members because workers are no longer as interchangeable as they once were. While job sharing is common, costly training is required to make employees more transferable. Technology has also brought with it some scary possibilities. Today it does not require large numbers of workers to bring production to a standstill; now one simple computer virus can stop a whole organization. The shift in power is virtually complete. From the master's dominance of workers and the unions' collective bargaining tactics and members' constraints, once again the individual has been freed. Employees have regained the power to be more creative and productive through knowledge and technology. The rise in individualism has created opportunities for collaboration between individuals, and between individuals and corporations. How we approach this challenge is going to be of major importance. These events and the sometimes-resulting chaos demand a review of current leadership styles and concepts with a goal to create new strategies, which can produce greater collaboration. The proliferation of technology is not an upheaval, but rather, it presents us with opportunities, which we should seize. In effect, we require new structures and strategies more appropriate to the changing environment. Alvin Toffler sustains this point of view:

> "It also implies a totally different power relationship between employer and employee. It means that intelligent error needs to be tolerated. Multitudes of bad ideas need to be floated and freely discussed, in order to harvest a single good one. And this implies a new, liberating freedom from fear." [2]

The creation of control through fear and the exercise of power has been the favorite strategy of management in the past. However, the need for innovative ideas and the speed to react to ever changing market forces is imperative. This new environment requires new strategies governed by freedom of the individual in the workplace. Fortunately, many organizations understand that innovation is driven by creativity and is usually fostered in less bureaucratic, hierarchical organizations. The future lies in organizations that embrace the freedom of employees to empower themselves and promote a new style of leadership, which fosters this corporate culture.

As mentioned earlier, the medieval style of secrecy and lack of information gave way to innovation and creativity in the more open era of the Renaissance. Similarly the bureaucratic and autocratic styles of management which resulted from the studies and theories of Henri Fayol and Frederick W. Taylor must, in many cases, be set aside. Old management concepts must give way to flexibility and participation, which are more conducive to our new renaissance created by the proliferation of technology and information. In addition, managers must realize that although many of the concepts of modern management have their origins in the West, there are many values from other cultures that can be incorporated to alleviate the constraints of current management practices. We can learn from different cultures how to adapt, respect our colleagues and manage with empathy.

Japanese culture imbues its people with values that facilitate teamwork. In recent years modified team concepts have been introduced into western organizations to facilitate team-based models. Although the more individualistic western values do not completely lend themselves to this approach, research shows that specialists and knowledge workers are embracing the mantra of teamwork. These highly skilled workers prefer the team concept instead of the more conventional hierarchical and pyramidal environment of bureaucratic organizations.

In the context of human resource management it is time to reexamine our current practices and put into place new strategies, which enable us to both move forward and at the same time provide more flexibility to the workforce. In this book I will propose that we embrace a new style of leadership in our organizations: a leadership which will make better use of all the organization's resources – material and human, and one based on collaboration and team work.

The concept of organizing workers into teams stems from the success of sports organizations. Very often coaching techniques and sports jargon are introduced to implement strategies within organizations. While there have been many benefits from the introduction of teams in organizations, unfortunately in many cases workers are still not buying entirely into the concept – perhaps for good reason. This lack of immediate enthusiasm stems from the loss of trust and the inability of management to embrace many of the philosophies that are used in team management in the sport arena.

When organizations fail, very often the initial reaction results in staff reduction, mainly lower and middle management employees. In sports, where the team concept originates, failures are usually the responsibility of the leader, that is; the coach. Although, players may be traded as a result of a failure, more often that not the coach is the one who suffers the consequences. One may sympathize with coaches, but in reality it is their inability to choose the right players, make proper use of their skills and implement the right strategies, that produce mediocre results. In short, it is their leadership shortcomings, which usually contribute to failure. A classic example is the 1995/96 St. Louis Blues hockey team, where Mike Keenan was fired from his coaching job after the team's failure in the Stanley Cup. Keenan had at his disposal a team made up of some of the best hockey players – Wayne Gretzky, Brett Hull, Al Macinnis, and Grant Fuhr to name but a few, nonetheless they did not win hockey's greatest prize. Many attributed the team's failure to the dictatorial style of the coach and to his inability to communicate with some of his star players.

While the team concept is an excellent means of changing organizations from a hierarchical to a flatter model, there are certain other concepts from the sport environment, which have not been fully integrated in its implementation. Too often, management is using the concept of teamwork to group individuals and makes it easier to assign blame collectively rather than individually. In many bureaucratic organizations, the team concept has not change things very much. Where middle managers are still in control they exert the same power, but now they do it by way of group manipulation. In these organizations, there is no intention to truly empower workers; it is still very much the same rhetoric that has been heard for generations. Consequently, there still exists a degree of skepticism in the minds of employees and they are unwilling and unable to fully embrace change. Workers today are looking for fairness in recognition and treatment of both their achievements and failures. Management often talks about workers as human assets; however there are still some organizations that still treat workers like chattels, which can quickly be disposed of. Organizations must adopt new strategies to maximize the use of employees or they run the risks of losing them very quickly. On the other hand workers must also recognize that the work environment has changed and that lifetime employment is a thing of the past.

In today's ever changing work environment workers must take into consideration that job security no longer exists. Most workers today can expect to work at least in five different careers before they retire – if they can afford to retire. Management must also recognize that workers' needs have also changed in recent years. It is no longer always the climb on the ladder of success that matters. Increasingly workers' needs include flexibility, quality family time, self-development and appropriate rewards – which are not always monetary.

We have reached a point in our history, where a clash between economic and social precepts is taking place at a rapid rate. In order to deal with the problems, which these events bring forth, as a society, we need new parameters and new solutions. As Alvin Toffler said:

> "In a time of exploding change – with personal lives being torn apart, the existing social order crumbling, and a fantastic new way of life emerging on the horizon – asking the very largest of questions about our future is not merely a matter of intellectual curiosity. It is a matter of survival."[3]

In this new era, new systems and structures, which can address these changes, are required. Any reform must be done with the involvement of all parties concerned. Hence the team concept. This book is not another set of ideas, which pretends to be the panacea for all management and organizational problems. Rather, it is an invitation for action to anybody who is interested in a rebuilding process to make organizations, institutions and in general people work together to solve the day-to-day drudgery of work and other social issues.

The rebuilding process is as follows:

Part One (Chapters 2-5) sets the parameters for the blue print design of this new structure. It looks at the forces of change, the role of culture in organizations, and the resulting consequences. The discussions of these issues automatically elicit the question: What's next?

Part Two (Chapters 6-10) provides the structure for this concept. It deals with the values and ideas that could be put in place to clearly involve people in teamwork. Leadership, as well as the elements of the team concept, which are the Four Pillars of our building are discussed. They are trust, empowerment, acceptance and motivation.

(Chapters 11-15) explains the five principles of Trust, which are so important for the achievement and success of any relationship. The four walls and the roof of our 'home' represent them.

Part Three (Chapters16-17) presents a new construction technique to build our home, made up of the four "Pillars" of Team and the four walls and roof of Trust. A number of proposals are put forward to achieve change and address problems in the new millennium. To face these new problems a new set of rules is required.

No longer can we just have an individual or a group of individuals formulate solutions for the collective. In a world where the number of educated and knowledge people is growing rapidly, these people must be given the opportunity to contribute to the organization which employs them and society at large. They cannot remain as followers; they must become contributors and masters of their destiny.

Leadership in this new era will take a different form. The dictatorial or paternalistic type of leader must take a back seat and make way for a more conciliatory style. The new leader will be one who embraces participation and fosters consensus. Collaboration is required at all levels to make things happen and provide the right solutions for a changing time. I hope that the ideas and the premise of this book provides an alternative choice which can make a difference in corporate life, and provide a platform which can be used by governments, unions and other institutions to resolve larger problems.

Part One

THE BLUE PRINT

CHAPTER 2

Change, the only constant

"When you can't change the direction of your wind – adjust your sails."
— Unknown.

THE BUZZ WORD of the nineties has been, and in the new century continues to be 'Change'. Every company, organization and business consultant talks about change. In the past decade, its impact on working conditions and lifestyles has been colossal and often daunting. Changes in technology, culture, relationships and the economy are at the center of the long self-examination being undertaken by individuals as well as organizations. The 'winds of change' are being felt everywhere.

The private sector has been at the forefront of change and the public sector can learn a lot from its successes and failures. Organizations in both the public and private sectors have consultants and administrative staff busy designing new strategies and implementing change. This trend is a response to the drivers of change, which must be discussed in order to understand what has been happening in most organizations over the past decade.

Drivers of Change

◆ **Economic Climate**
The early nineties were plagued by an economic recession, which barely subsided in 1994. All the major industrialized countries have seen their economic base eroded. In these hard economic times the word 'taxes' has taken a new meaning. They are no longer just feared and hated by the taxpayer, but have become the focus of some governments. All levels of government are being forced to look at alternative ways of doing things instead of raising taxes to pay for services. Federal governments are cutting grants to lower governments. Health and education and other social services costs are being trimmed. These changes have resulted in massive job and service cuts in the public sector and governments are, largely, no longer seen as the creators of jobs.

◆ **Debts and deficits** – All levels of government have accumulated large amounts of debt. Due to the recent recession it is feared that countries can no longer manage their economy in the same old fashion. It is no longer acceptable, fashionable – or in some cases, feasible – to continue deficit financing by the public sector. The United States faces a $16 trillion debt and other countries do not fare better.

◆ **Globalization** – Many trade barriers are falling. Through agreements such as the World Trade Organization (WTO), trade between most industrialized countries has increased. Mergers and acquisitions are no longer confined to national boundaries; they continue to occur across national frontiers. Joint ventures and strategic alliances are common occurrences in the new global environment.

◆ **Unemployment** – No longer is unemployment solely the plague of the less developed nations. In the mid-90s the industrialized countries of the world experienced the highest level of unemployment since the pre-World War II depression. In 2012 the United States experienced unemployment rates of 7%-8%.

◆ **Technology** – A shift in work methods and communication channels is being created by technology. Information is more readily available and technology creates a new breed of employees who are more knowledgeable and less likely to operate under the same conditions of the hierarchies of old management styles.

In the new century, we have seen an increase in e-commerce. This new business platform is driven by the growing use of the internet as a business tool. The only barriers to growth in e-commerce, may well be consumers' lack of trust in the security system and possible government regulation. Fortunately, in 1997, in what can be seen as a break through legal decision, U.S. Federal District Court Judge Marylin Hall Patel of San Francisco ruled that:

> *"the encryption regulations are an unconstitutional prior restraint in violation of the First Amendment."*

This decision has in effect deregulated the Internet market for security, thus allowing the use of virtually unbreakable codes to be used to protect consumers' privacy and security. Optimism remains high that governments will stay away from over regulating this form of business. In fact, the United States would like to see e-commerce operate as a new free market for goods and services, while the EEC took a different view on security encoding – which may prevent free trade between EEC members and the rest of the world. The EEC's legislation may prevent the proliferation of e-commerce and may also be contrary to WTO rules on free trade.

♦ **Urban Poverty** – More industrialized nations are finding that poverty in their major cities is putting enormous stress on their ability to provide social welfare programs. As many cities become more prosperous, more people migrate to them. While jobs are available, there is a growing crisis to find affordable housing. With this situation comes not only homelessness, but also growing urban problems due to unforeseen and rapid growth. Infrastructures become insufficient and certain types of crime may be on the rise.

♦ **Demographics** – The larger aging population is increasing demand for health care services, while urban youth are finding it more difficult to find jobs. Concurrent with the growing GenX population comes new demands and the creation of new markets. The demographics of South East Asia also bode well for the future. India and China now boast the fastest growing middle-class. Should the economic situation in Asia change for the better; there is enormous potential for trade in that region.

♦ **Competition** – Among cities, provinces/states and nations competition is growing. To increase their economic bases and prop up their dwindling revenues these levels of government are getting more competitive in attracting new businesses to their jurisdictions. Technology increasingly enables the conduct of business from smaller centers. Smaller cities with less urban problems, such as traffic and crime continue to attract more businesses. The other side of this coin is that there are areas, which are losing businesses and are facing the problems of high unemployment.

The Effects of Globalization

Of the several drivers of change listed above, globalization has the largest impact on how businesses and governments operate in the next millennium. Information technology and the information superhighway has enhanced the speed at which business transactions are done.

The movement of capital funds around the world continues to accelerate and create many economic opportunities as well as cause economic turmoil rarely seen in previous years. As exemplified by the recent collapse of major banks in the United States which was followed by a world economic recession. It is no longer possible to manage individual national economies without taking economic events in other countries seriously and from a global perspective. National economies are entwined to the extent that international policies make more sense today.

Organizations and agreements such as The G20, the EEC and North American Free Trade Agreement have taken an increasing role in the management of the world economy. While the International Monetary Fund has played a major role in trying to help solve some of these problems, increasing government debt remains the biggest concern.

We also see a growing trend in activities by non-government organizations (NGO), Unions and other environmental groups. These groups' activities range from the presentations of research papers to demonstrations accompanied by violence, the later activities more so than the former. Demonstrations, and riots in both Seattle in 1999 and Washington D.C in 2000 are examples of this trend, followed more recently by the so called 'Occupy Movement'.

Governments, corporations and labor unions must approach the new challenges of a globalized economy in a totally different way. It is no longer possible to manage today's events with yesterday's management tools.

Why Change?

In essence we need change to provide the needed services to customers in a more efficient and effective manner. Organizations have to be more competitive and provide added value, usually at the same, if not lower, costs. In so doing these corporations, which have operated within a bureaucratic structure have learned and are continuing to learn to change in order to adapt to the new circumstances imposed upon them by the drivers of change. Organizations will have to support their existence by the provision of quality service and the development of mutual respect with their clients. In this respect, five areas of concern are illustrated by Philippe Roy (1990-91) who stated that:

> "Strategic new direction in quality and service must build on five essential components: 1. Leadership, 2. Marketing management,

3. Organizational change and development, 4. Human resource management, and 5. Relationship management." [1]

The remainder of this chapter discusses these components and looks at strategies, which are being used to bring forth change in both the private and public sectors

Reinventing Government

Over the years the role of government has changed. Bureaucratic organizations with thousands of civil servants have become the managers, if not the rulers, of our lives. The title of 'civil servants' is certainly an ironic paradox in this era. The bureaucrats have long forgotten that their function is to 'serve' the citizens, who are the taxpayers hence, their employers. The bureaucrats have taken their role to a different level. Through their self-directed, unchallenged policies and procedures they have become the rulers of the land. In the guise of advisors to the politicians, they have taken up the mantle of 'mandarins' who are effectively the policy-makers. In this role they have learned to pander to the whims of politicians and interest groups. They are so busy climbing the stairs of success and prestige that they have forgotten their true role – to serve the citizens.

E.S. Savas (1987), consultant and author of **Privatization: The Key to Better Government**, remarked:

> "The word government is from a Greek word, which means, "to steer."
> The job of government is to steer, not to row the boat. Delivering services is rowing and government is not very good at rowing."

The reinvention of government demands that these organizations work in a new way. Governments must be judged by their ability to do more with less. The new circumstances require quality of services for less tax. They should be required to be out of the business of being sole providers; they must now become facilitators and encourage competition between themselves and other providers of services. Consequently, governments must concentrate on 'rowing' instead of 'steering.'

In many American cities this process is already taking place. Communities are being given more say in what and how services will be delivered. Communities are gradually being empowered to make decisions, which directly affect them. At the same time, it is clear, and to be fair, entrepreneurial governments can successfully compete against private enterprise for services which they used to run under monopolistic environments. In many instances they are winning contracts against the best of the private sector. ". As Gaebler, and Osborne (1992) explained:

"They measure the performance of their agencies, focusing not on inputs but on *outcomes*. They are driven by their goals – their *missions* – not by their rules and regulations. They redefine their clients as *customers* and offer them choices – . . ."[2]

The new reality dictates that government reinvents itself; that is, get out of the business of being all things to all people. Instead of being a provider of all services, it should become the facilitator for the provision of services at the lowest cost. Governments at all levels should concentrate on ways to earn money, not on devising ways and means to spend it.

Re-engineering

As a strategy for change, re-engineering seems to have been the favored method. Hammer.M and Champy.J (1993) define reengineering as:

"The fundamental rethinking and radical redesign of business processes to achieve dramatic improvements in critical, contemporary measures of performance, such as cost, quality, service and speed."[3]

It encompasses all the necessary tactics that may be needed to effectively reach the goals of change. Re-engineering is not the same as Total Quality Management (TQM), although it may involve TQM. Reengineering requires several additional concepts to be successful.

Many organizations have reinvented themselves, or are in the process of doing so and reengineering has provided the methodology for that change. It requires starting all over again from the beginning. This exercise usually requires the re-examination of the organization's business, and the identification of what should stay and what processes should be changed to achieve improvements in services, delivery and speed. There are three precepts used to achieve reengineering: Reposition, Reconfigure, and Restructure.

Reposition

In order to change, a business must be able to look at itself and see if its operations are correctly positioned within the market. Both private and public sector organizations must reposition many of their activities. In the public sector, examples of this include activities, which can be outsourced or provided for by means of partnerships between government and the private sector. Similarly, the private sector has used outsourcing and the transfer of production to countries where labor is cheaper.

Reconfigure

Because bureaucratic culture in organizations usually slows down processes, it is important to reconfigure processes to create a smoother workflow. Reconfiguration in organizations has seen the removal of many existing process barriers which prevent the smooth delivery of services. Processes have been altered and improved, with an increased focus on the big issues of quality, added values and lower costs.

Restructure

Bureaucratic organizations are almost always too segmented, constraining the speed of delivery. Controls abound and slow down the process. Too many people are required to manage such a structure. Empowerment is needed to allow employees to make their own rules instead of following rules. Employees must use flexibility, learning experiences and common sense to contribute more fully to their organizations. With reengineering, the rules change. Generalists can do the work of experts. Decision-making is everybody's business, information flows freely across all levels, pay for performance and results become the norm and bonuses, and not pay raises are the rewards of these organizations. The search for reengineering opportunities often leads to the examination of processes often hidden by organizational structures. To effectively reach the goals of reengineering, it is necessary to restructure organizations to remove the barriers of hierarchy, segmentalism and overkill control, which exist in bureaucratic organizations.

Total Quality Management

Since the West learned of the success of Japan's use of TQM, there has been a rush by private and public sector organizations to embrace this concept. TQM, ironically, was taken to Japan after the WWII by management theorist W. Edwards Deming, of the United States of America. Around the early 80s, it was rediscovered by western organizations after nearly two decades of taking an economic beating by the Japanese. First embraced by the private sector, TQM is gradually filtering its way into the public sector.

The experience of TQM in many organizations supports the idea of opportunities for employee participation as well as the acquisition of knowledge and growth from mutual exchange of ideas. The fundamental concept of TQM is the creation of competitive advantage by focusing the organization and its resources on what is important to the customer. As a tactic, when TQM is fully implemented in an organization it has the potential of completely transforming not only the service delivery but also the entire structure and culture of an organization.

Transformational change occurs when both strategic management and strategic leadership are carried out successfully. Nutt, Paul.C, Backoff, Robert. W (1993) contend that

> "TQM provides a way to connect both strategic management and leadership, through self managed work groups, through massive delegation and empowerment to make changes".[4]

However, we must also be aware that TQM may not be the panacea that most gurus of change purport it to be. Some doubt that TQM is the complete answer for the public sector. The limitations of TQM can be found in the stress that is put on product rather than services, on input and processes rather than results, and its inherent strong preoccupation with quality.

Daniel Niven (1993) contends that TQM programs of the 80s will have to be reviewed in light of the downsizing trends of the 90s. Bad execution may be the reason why TQM has failed in as many as two-thirds of American companies surveyed. In a survey of North American and European companies, McKinsey found that 67 percent of TQM programs older than two years die due to a lack of results (Globe and Mail Report on Business Magazine Nov.1992). Despite these reports of failures and our acknowledgment that there are barriers and difficulties to be overcome, the general consensus is that, properly implemented, TQM can beneficially serve many organizations both in the public and private sectors.

Recipe for TQM success

There are specific ingredients required to make TQM successful. These ingredients, like spices in cooking, will turn a good dish into a gourmet one. The blend of spices which TQM brings with its implementation are the catalyst for the sauce of change.

The ingredients required are:

- **Total support of top management**, not just the rhetoric of values and beliefs published in 'corporate communications', but ***true commitment*** to a program which brings senior management in contact with individual employees.
- **Customer-focus** which starts in-house, where all employees feel that their colleagues are their customers. This attitude will be reflected in the staff's dealing with the ultimate customer, the public.

- **Long-term strategic plans** which enables the employee and the organization to work towards long-term goals instead of the shorterminism attitude, which prevails in most Western organizations.
- **Employee training and recognition** that provides every member of staff with the necessary tools to provide the best service possible. In return the organization must provide appropriate and adequate recognition for the achievements of its employees.
- **Employee empowerment and teamwork** is at the center of successful TQM programs. Bureaucratic obstacles must be removed to allow the exchange of ideas between colleagues and across departmental borders. Segmentalist attitudes must be extinguished in order to bring employees together in teams that can better contribute to the organization.
- **Measurement of performance** is required in order to track the progress of the program and in order to provide guidelines for future decisions. Benchmarking and new accounting methods are required. Data collection must be more meaningful and accessible to all. There is a role for the true accountant to play in this new era. Willis George (1991) said:

> "To implementation teams, the accountant brings to bear measurement and reporting skills, knowledge of clients, services and available resources, and a broad-based perspective on organizational issues."[5]

- **Quality assurance** to the customer that the quality of services will be maintained, if not improved, and linked to likely to lower costs to provide those services.
- **Union participation** is a key to the success of TQM in unionized environments. Employees as well as unions must be involved in developing measurement and reporting systems, redesign of processes, compensation, performance evaluation and training and development systems.

TQM has so much potential for change, and participation is at the center of its success. Unfortunately, it can easily fail if the commitment of all parties is not sought or obtained. Supportive leadership is absolutely essential to drive the changes needed to effectively implement the program.

Cultural Change

The introduction of reengineering has the potential to fundamentally alter the fabric of an organization. Change will take different forms and will range from a total cultural change as a result of reinventing, restructuring, downsizing and perhaps demassing *(demassing will be explained later)*. Each of these consequences of change must be examined in order to understand the implementation strategies, which have been used by organizations in the past decade.

Before the gains resulting from the implementation of re-engineering are achieved, there is usually, at the initiation stage, a large amount of pain associated with early retirement, lay-offs, transfers, performance appraisals, rewards & punishment and change in lifestyle. All change brings with it stress and resistance. Cultural change is no exception.

Downsizing, Demassing

In a restructured and reengineered organization, many processes and layers of management and staff positions disappear. How this unenviable task is undertaken is very important to the morale of the remaining staff and the culture. As for those who are let go, it is important that they are treated fairly.

Downsizing is less harsh on the organization. When processes have been redesigned only those affected by the change will be let go. Cutbacks due to reduced activity require layoffs in smaller numbers. Demassing on the other hand requires a large number of redundancies, usually larger than 10 percent of the workforce. Demassing does not have to take place if an orderly and planned restructuring strategy is used. This solution can have grave consequences on corporate morale and can create social problems by dumping a large number of people on welfare and social services support.

What we have seen so far are the current methods employed to implement change. However, as we shall see in Chapter 4, the methodology and consequences of implementation have not been as successful as we may have been led to believe. In fact, in many cases it has ended in chaos and harsh results, which are affecting the very fabric of work relationships and causing socio-economic problems. What is required is a better-planned strategy to implement change, one that will cause the minimum of stress to and within the organization and yet produce the best results.

Restructuring is not so simple as we may have been lead to believe. Why do so many of today's organizations find it so difficult to reach their full potential? For a start, over the years I have observed that much of the past failures have been the result of having the wrong . . .

CHAPTER 3

Corporate Culture

"Culture is not something that you manipulate easily."
– John P. Kotter.

IN ORDER TO examine cultural change in any organization, we must first understand the meaning of corporate culture. We shall look at the origins of corporate culture, how it is developed and sustained, and how it contributes or hinders corporate performance. In addition, we shall discuss different organization structures and different cultures with links between different types of corporate cultures and how they fit in different organizations. The measurement of culture is extremely difficult, but it is important to have some methodology to assess culture in order to measure the effectiveness of any change undertaken.

Definition and Origins of Corporate Culture

Peters and Waterman first popularized the notion of corporate culture in their book *In Search of Excellence*, a product of their research of successful U.S. corporations. They identified eight characteristics, which contributed to the success of these corporations. Since then there have been much research work and numerous books written on the subject of corporate culture and it has become a widely accepted criteria for the measurement of success within the corporate world encompassing both the private and public sectors. From a historical perspective, the private sector was quick to embrace the theory of cultural change while the public sector was slow to even recognize its existence.

> *Webster's New Collegiate Dictionary* defines culture, as "the integrated pattern of human behavior that includes thought, speech, action, and artifacts and depends on man's capacity for learning and transmitting knowledge to succeeding generations."

For our purposes, in the context of corporations, a more appropriate definition would be the one supplied by Marvin Bower (1980) in *The Will to Manage* – **"the way we do things around here."**

If we combine these two definitions, we can get closer to an understanding of corporate culture and the factors that influence and shape it. In a national culture it takes leaders and the willingness of followers to shape a culture. Together they provide and create myths, histories, values, rites and rituals, artifacts, and heroes.

Similarly, in corporate culture we have the same elements. We need leaders who are prepared to set values and goals, and followers who are willing to accept those values and goals as their own. Communication therefore plays an important role in the dissemination and acceptance of ideas among a group of people, in this case the employees of a firm. A strong culture provides an effective vehicle to control behavior. Control happens in the consolidation stages of a culture, when people have bought into the system and leadership moves towards putting into place strategies, structures and systems. What happens at the consolidation stage is very important. It can create a strong culture, which in turn can create problems of inflexibility, which may in the long-term cause the downfall of the culture. It is almost certain to happen if the control is so stringent and the culture so strong that under evolving and revolutionary circumstances the members of the culture are not flexible enough to adapt and change adequately.

Organization Structures

An effective discussion on organization culture cannot be accomplished without an understanding of organization structures. For the purposes of our discussions we shall identify the two main and contrasting types of organizational structure, specifically the hierarchical versus the flatter structures.

The hierarchical structure is usually represented by the shape of a pyramid, with the seat of authority and control at the very top and the diminishing layers of command gradually filling the space below. Much of the philosophies within this structure are based on old management theories, which were used in the early stages of the industrial revolution. Management theorists like Fayol and Taylor were very supportive of this type of management structure. The division of labor and skills was at the heart of these structures. It was believed that workers should focus on what they have to do and managers would dictate the policies and procedures for workers to implement. The hierarchies and different levels of this structure are commonly known as a bureaucracy. With its levels of departments, divisions and sub-divisions, this structure is frequently found in governments and until recently, in most large corporations.

The more open and flatter organization structures originate from the 'contingency approach' a concept based on theories that have emerged more recently. The rise of this approach can be attributed to increasing global competition and the need of corporations to react very quickly. This theory takes into consideration that corporations not only consists of tasks/processes that have to be performed but also require people to accomplish them. As a consequence this approach requires that organizations seek a 'fit' between tasks and processes, people, and their environment. This fit will obviously be contingent upon the prevailing circumstances that include the insight and skills of management. This new organizational approach in itself provides for flexibility. Organizations, which use the concepts of this theory, are usually flatter, less bureaucratic and generally more conscious of the value of teamwork. They are structured more horizontally than vertically. They also recognize that customers do not care about the structure of the organizations, but care about the one-on-one relationship they have with their immediate corporate contact.

Types of Culture

Different organizations need different types of cultures. The type of culture required to implement change will be an important factor. Deal & Kennedy (1982), identified four generic cultures:

- **"The tough-guy, macho culture.** A world of individualists who regularly take high risks and get quick feedback on whether their actions were right or wrong."
- **"The work hard /play hard culture.** Fun and action are the rule here, and employees take few risks, all with quick feedback; to succeed, the culture encourages them to maintain a high level of relatively low-risk activity."
- **"The bet-your-company culture.** Cultures with big-stakes decisions, where years pass before employees know whether decisions have paid off. A high-risk, slow-feedback environment."
- **"The process culture.** A world of little or no feedback where employees find it hard to measure what they do; instead they concentrate on how it's done. We have another name for this culture when the processes get out of control bureaucracy!"

The culture of an organization may contain sub-cultures depending on the activities of the sub-culture.

For example the sales and marketing division of a company may have the culture associated with the "work hard/play hard" classification, while the research & development division will reflect a "bet your company" culture and the accounting department more likely have a "process culture". However, the dominant culture will be determined by the goals, objectives and values of the organization. To be more effective the chosen culture should be supported by mission statements and mottos which continuously remind employees of these objectives.

Climate and Environment

The right climate and environment must exist in order to enable the change process in a corporation. Rosabeth Moss-Kanter has written about the concept of segmentalist and integrative cultures. Her premise is that each culture and environment has a different effect on the process of change.

Segmentalism

The segmentalist type of culture is usually one where change is not encouraged and innovation is not a priority. This type of culture is prevalent in bureaucratic structures. It promotes actions in isolation, and has a fragmented type of structure. This encourages employees to work within set boundaries, often preventing the sharing of ideas between people within the same area and let alone across divisions or departments. This culture works under the rigor of procedures and regulations and usually creates massive amounts of 'red tape'.

Secrecy and confidentiality – even about the simplest things – rather than open communication are the norm. Inflexibility is prevalent and the rules and procedures are often used as a pretext to fight initiative. This brings me to recall an incident I was involved in while working as an accountant for the City of Calgary. At one stage I was responsible to prepare the budget for a contingency account, which included amounts pertaining to possible wage settlements under collective agreements. Since they were computed before any discussions with the unions, it was very confidential. A year after preparing the budget I was transferred to another position. Sometime later during another research project I needed to access this contingency account. When I asked for the information I had compiled for the figures, I was informed that they were confidential and no longer available to me. Although these figures, originally prepared by me had not changed, I had to go and ask permission through the proper channel that is through my manager, to finally obtain them.

This type of environment is usually one where 'back stabbing' takes place frequently. Employees tend to be judged by others and management is quick to condemn the actions of employees. Praise is infrequent or virtually inexistent. Frequently organizations, which espouse the segmentalist culture, are also the same ones that experience problems in the areas of discrimination and cover-ups. Because control is exercised at all levels, many problems are not brought to the surface or are covered up by different levels of management. This results from a climate of fear and lack of support from higher ups. In many cases in this type of climate when a problem arises most believe it is better to keep quiet than to bring it to the fore. The culture does not support the messenger, but rather deals with problems by 'shooting the messenger' and ignoring the message. This environment perpetuates rather than solves problems.

The design of the organizational structure is based on the typical pyramid, with absolute control at the top and very little say at the bottom. Management is usually self-righteous believing it knows it all. In this case suggestions or input from employees are not requested, rarely tolerated and almost never accepted and/or implemented. These organizations have typically been the greatest users of the re-engineering, re-organizing and downsizing trends of recent past. Many have not attempted to alter their culture but are in the process of doing further reorganizations to address their continuing problems.

Integrative

The integrative style is one, which encourages innovation, the sharing of ideas across the organization. It provides a climate that promotes harmony and enables decisions to be made across divisional and departmental boundaries. Moss Kanter, (1983) stated:

> "Integrative thinking that actively embraces change is more likely in companies whose cultures and structures are also integrative, encouraging the treatment of problems as 'wholes,' considering the wider implications of actions." [2]

Corporations, which embrace the contingency theory, are the ones that frequently adopt an integrative culture. They also tend to promote communication at all levels and encourage learning and retraining. In simple terms they are more effective at finding a fit between people, processes and their environment. As a result they become more flexible and able to make rapid changes to respond to the needs of the market and competition.

Organizations with an integrative culture tend to have flatter structures with less managerial hierarchies. The use of employee suggestions, without bias, is commonly used and often encouraged. The open environment allows for open discussions between employees of different levels and encourages initiative and creativity. Risk taking is encouraged, and mistakes are viewed as a stepping stone towards success rather than failure.

The Importance of Culture

In today's new environment more organizations will find themselves increasingly and constantly affected by information technology. Computers, social media and ease of access to information have become clear agents of cultural change. In many cases, the amount of data that can be manipulated and stored in computers has reduced much of the paper shuffling required by past processes. Since less paper work is required and more information is made available to a larger number of people within an organization, it seems clear that less hierarchy is required. It is therefore possible and desirable to flatten large bureaucratic organizations as the layers of management required to transmit policies and procedures down the pyramid becomes less important. When organizations get flatter there is also the need to redefine the roles of management. For instance, the roles of manager and supervisor change to facilitator and coach. In a flatter organization the proper culture makes it possible for the decision maker to relate more to the establishment of corporate strategic goals. In turn the managers cease to be data collectors and transmitters of orders and focus their activities on developing and motivating employees. In essence, the flatter organization requires leaders who can visualize long-term strategies and select the right people to implement them. The other levels of management are responsible for the operational implementation and require managers to have the ability to motivate, lead and coach the employees responsible to implement the objectives of the corporation.

Globalization is ever increasing and we must not ignore its effect on organization culture. So far we have discussed culture in the internal context of an organization. However, we must not forget that culture also transcends national boundaries. Corporations doing business in foreign countries must be cognizant of other national cultures. Leaders in a globalized environment will have to acquire skills which include the ability to manage in different countries and cultures because clearly there will be a demand for competencies which transcends national cultures.

Blending Cultures

With increasing mergers and acquisitions, alliances and joint ventures, there will be a need for the ability to blend cultures. Very often when two corporations merge, the priorities are the financial and strategic benefits. However corporate culture, despite being regarded as an important management issue in these amalgamations, is very often ignored or implemented accidentally. What usually happens in these circumstances is that companies often unintentionally tinker with the culture of newly acquired firms. In so doing they can destroy the very characteristics which made the merger attractive in the first place. By imposing new rules or removing some of the rituals, which made the acquired company successful, they can easily and unwittingly destroy morale or the entrepreneurial spirit of the workforce. When a merger occurs, it is very important that culture be put at or near the very top of the agenda. It is important to be able to evaluate, assess the values and benefits of corporate culture. In this context successful cultural attributes of both companies should be identified. Management should then define the specifics of the culture and communicate them to everyone in the new corporation. This important step in a merger or acquisition will have critical implications on the structure of the company, and how the two companies blend and perform in the future.

Measurement of Change

The measurement of change is very difficult because it requires the assessment of many interdependent factors. Professor Roy Payne of the United Kingdom has discussed the problems associated with measuring change. He contends that a proper measurement of culture must include the assessment of both the explicit and implicit culture. He states that the assessment of 'climate' may be a measurement of explicit culture, and not a way of measuring implicit culture. In 1976, Payne R.L and Pugh D.S, define 'climate' as:

> "a molar *(acting on large masses or units)* concept reflecting the content and strength of the prevalent values, norms, attitudes, behaviors and feelings of members of a social system".

On the other hand Payne, (1991) identifies implicit culture as:

> "The proportion of the members of a social group that firmly holds to the norms and beliefs."[3]

The success of companies will be determined by the strength of their culture and the cohesion, which exist within the organization. Employees within successful companies will strongly identify themselves with the goals and objectives of the company while forming a strong bond among themselves to achieve these goals. The shape of the corporate culture will be determined by the amount of risk associated with the company's activities and the speed by which feedback is given to employees about their contribution to the decision-making strategy and goals achieved.

If the stage is set for the organization of tomorrow, it must get away from the bureaucratic and autocratic cultures based on military hierarchy and chain of command. Instead, the current trend is a movement towards organizations that embrace the 'contingency theory' management style where employees are treated as partners rather than performers of tasks and where the culture promotes working together rather than working for somebody.

In the following chapters I will discuss how we can structure the organization of tomorrow to accommodate a better fit between people, processes and environment. However the choice of a strategy to create a better work environment will be greatly affected if we do not understand the potential . . .

CHAPTER 4

Consequences

"The future has a way of arriving unannounced."
— George F. Will.

"Most layoffs at large companies have been the fault of managers who
fell asleep at the wheel and missed the turnoff for the future."
C.K. Prahalad.

THE PRESSURES OF corporate change started in the early eighties and have continued to grow and corporations have intensified their reengineering strategies to become more competitive.

Despite the best intentions, this trend has caused enormous harm, which has been felt by many employees. In some industrialized countries, unemployment lines continue to grow. A major difference this time is that not only blue-collar workers are affected but layoffs among white-collar workers has seen a marked increase.

After WWII and during the short economic lows of the sixties and early seventies, it was customary to see corporations lay off blue-collar workers while management workers on the other hand felt very safe. With the advent of technology this situation has changed drastically to the point that blue-collar workers' jobs are becoming somewhat safer than management workers' positions. Compared to blue-collar workers who have the protection of their unions, white-collar workers have become more vulnerable. Increasingly in the 90s, corporations have restructured themselves to the detriment of middle management, which is now viewed as expendable since computers can do most of their work. At least that is the point of view taken by top management. In fact there are no guarantees any more, as Horton and Reid (1991) say:

> "No more guarantees of lifetime employment. No more automatic salary increases. No more promotions for just showing up. No more bankable career ladders. The unwritten contract between employers and their middle managers that promised all those things is dead and buried." [1]

The winds of change have brought with them many new problems and consequences and in order to remedy the current situation it is wise to examine the effects which change has brought forward. Through downsizing, restructuring and reengineering corporations have brought upon society a number of problems ranging from economic to psychological. Susan and Thomas Kuczmarski (1995) observed:

> "The current state of our work organizations perpetuates a feeling of helplessness on the part of most and an attitude of entrapment for many. Today many employees feel isolated, deceived, and alienated at work. Nothing personal, nothing emotional, and certainly nothing meaningful. They literally don't believe in their work." [2]

Why did this happen? Today's morale crisis in the workplaces of the industrialized world cannot be solved without a serious look at these consequences and their affects. The objective of this examination is to isolate these consequences and identify the possible reasons for their advent. It is only then that we can attempt to rectify and improve the current situation.

Economics

During the boom years after WWII, there was no holding back economic growth. During this era of prosperity other perks that today are taken for granted became commonplace. As a result most workers felt that their jobs were secured for life. It was common for people to join a company after school or college and work with the same corporation until retirement. With this understanding there came an unwritten agreement that for work performed there will be steady incremental wage increases, promotions to the next level of the hierarchy and a retirement funded by the employer or jointly by the employee and the employer. In addition there were other benefits, which included health and dental care and even life insurance in certain circumstances. This unwritten covenant was not only held between employer and white-collar workers, but also held between blue-collar workers and the employer through the bargaining agreements made on their behalf by their unions.

All in all, this arrangement was quite satisfactory to both parties and the cozy understanding between management and workers went on until the oil crisis of the 70s. This was effectively the first economic shock wave to hit industrialized countries since WWII, and it hit hard. When the price of oil went up, many adjustments had to be made. The automobile industry had to restructure itself to adapt their products to the increasing cost of fuel. To cut costs corporations started to cut back on certain benefits to workers, and the relationship between unions and management started to sour. As industrial strife grew, management decided to cut back on staff costs by laying off blue-collar workers. To gain or maintain economies of scale many corporations initiated mergers or acquisitions. With this came further layoffs of workers and it was mostly blue-collar workers who were affected. White-collar workers, with some exceptions, were spared from layoffs. Even when they were laid off, white-collar workers found it fairly easy to find suitable employment elsewhere.

In the 80s, however the first cracks in the unwritten contract between white-collar workers and management started to appear. No longer was any job secured for life, with white-collar workers laid off with virtual impunity. Middle managers became an endangered species as their functions were downsized and outsourced. Thousands were laid off or given the option of early retirement. One aspect of this reduction in staff was that with every restructuring and downsizing, the unwritten contract was being violated and the most important tenet of the contract: "good performance in your job, will secure you a job for life", was consistently broken by management. It became clear the layoffs were not related to performance at all, but rather to the corporation's bottom line.

Methodology

It is a sad truth that in the nineties, the layoff of middle management became a desperate measure rather than a strategic activity. Reengineering, accompanied by downsizing and sometimes demassing became the norm for corporations in industrialized countries. For executives involved in this major change it was not a very difficult exercise and the financial markets applauded their actions. Management goals moved from long-term strategies to an emphasis on short-term objectives, focusing on quarterly financial results, shareholders' return on investment, and dividends.

The reasons for this change in management resulted from several factors. Firstly, ownership of major corporations has changed. Today most of the shares in large corporations are no longer held by individual shareholders but by large institutions and pension funds. These new shareholders have enormous clout and influence on the financial markets and they tend to dictate the short-term policies of executives. To satisfy these highly demanding new shareholders, management has seen fit to cut costs to increase earning per share by using downsizing as a strategic tool to reach their goals

The result has been felt mostly by white-collar workers and to a lesser extent by blue-collar workers who are still under some protection by being members of unions. However, even this security blanket is gradually being removed, as corporations move their manufacturing activities to foreign countries where they can find cheaper and usually non-unionized labor.

The second factor was global competition. For many years industrialized countries believed that there was no effective competition for their goods and services. When other countries, specifically Japan and the so-called Asian Tigers started to gain a foothold in the domestic market of industrialized countries it became apparent that those countries had to react with great speed to become more competitive. The task was daunting. The newcomers were competing with the advantages of lower labor costs and the benefit of a different more productive work ethic and culture. As the rest of the world caught up with the industrialized world, corporations realized they had to react faster and become more efficient by removing layers of management and downsizing was used to both save money and improve competitiveness. Cutting payroll costs instead of improving systems became the preferred methodology in the search for increased competitiveness. Technological advances in computerization made it possible to make do with fewer people, especially middle managers. Access to information became easier and therefore bosses responsible for passing down information became obsolete. The old unwritten contract contained huge benefit costs, and as they skyrocketed due to union demands under collective agreements and mandating by governments corporations found it easier and cheaper to hire contract and temporary workers who are not entitled to these benefits.

Survivor Shock

When downsizing takes place, often attention and sympathy is focused on those who are laid off and quite rightly so. However, in the aftermath of restructuring management rarely acknowledge that there is another side to their action. Under these circumstances, we should pay more attention to the survivors' reactions to management's new demands. Unfortunately after downsizing management usually reads the Riot Act to the survivors. New tasks and assignments are allocated willy-nilly, often accompanied by management's rhetoric that the corporation will treat you well when the situation improves. In the modern world, however, survivors very rarely see any improvement in their pay cheque, what they usually forced to accept is more work for less pay.

Survivors of downsizing are no less subject to fear, anxiety, and anger than those employees who were let go. Initially they may feel good about still having a job, but very quickly they start thinking that if it happened to somebody else, it can also happen to them. In many cases the sense of fear starts to grip their every free moment and they can no longer focus on the job at hand, because anxiety starts to settle in. They work longer hours because jobs have been downloaded onto them, and they get fewer benefits as the corporation continues to cut costs. Survivors very often get angry at the system that still provides them with a job but which continues to effectively decrease their salaries and/or benefits.

Corporate Loss

The result of this anxiety and pressure on survivors is clearly damaging to corporations. Survivors of downsizing adopt a different attitude towards corporate management becoming less loyal to their employer, withholding information for fear of being the bearer of bad news, and ceasing to contribute new ideas. Managers become risk averse for fear of being blamed and being laid off for making a mistake. The once good team player becomes a mercenary who is awaiting the next crisis, when she or he will be put out of a job and have to seek new surroundings for her or his skills. Employed survivors are often on the lookout to get to another corporation to protect their employability. Loyalty to their current employer or corporation has disappeared.

In many instances of downsizing, little planning takes place and fewer and fewer employees are laid off because of poor performance. The real reasons are usually for economic or cultural reasons. Managers who are in their 50s and earning between $60,000 and $80,000 are often the target for downsizing because economically they have become a burden to the corporation – their salaries and benefits are considered too high. Corporations believe they can hire contract or part time workers for less or without having to contribute any other benefits. The other facet of downsizing is that many people who are let go are released because they no longer fit the culture of the organization. In bureaucratic organizations, those who are laid off are usually those workers who challenge the status quo, often creative people who want to make changes to the system. These people are often let go by management because they are a threat to the hierarchical system and managers who are fearful of competition. When cultural differences are used to downsize, the corporation is left with a shell filled with the same type of people. The lack of diversity almost always prohibits creativity and innovation.

Where downsizing is accompanied by voluntary packages and voluntary early retirement the effect of the corporation can be disastrous. Under these circumstances the best people often take the packages and leave the company. These employees are commonly the 'intrapreneurs' of the organization, the creative ones who can no longer work within the culture or are ready to move on because their talents are not appreciated.

As employees become more disposable, the corporate environment becomes less inviting. Many downsized employees return to work for corporations, but in ever increasing numbers many do not. The downsized managers, nowadays seek to become self employed, sell their skills as consultants, often because they fear to be downsized once again if they accept a corporate position. They refuse to place themselves in positions where they can become vulnerable once again. The frustrations and anger of these executives and managers often convince them not to seek employment with large corporations. They can no longer trust the hierarchy and the culture of these large corporations. Today, these workers want to belong to organizations where a 'pat on the back' does not involve a sharp object. As a result these often bright and creative people with business acumen, know-how and expertise are no longer available to large corporations. Fear has not stopped young entrepreneurs from embracing e-com. In fact many successful executives are jumping ship from old to new economy companies Some examples of this migration from large corporations to more open organizations, specifically dot.com companies can be seen below:

I.   Brian Swetle from Pepsi Cola to eBay
II. Richard Namula from Starwood to Broadband

By creating a hostile, untrustworthy work environment corporations are slowly but surely depriving themselves of highly talented and valuable assets. Younger entrepreneurs are seeking companies with culture differences and work in organizations where they have the ability to contribute and grow.

The Career Ladder

Once upon a time in the corporate world, going up the ladder was believed to be the way to success. In these times of reengineering this belief has changed. As downsizing and often demassing takes place several managerial levels disappear. Usually left are the executive suite, lower management and rank-and-file workers. In these organizations there is little prospect for lower management employees to move up. For those workers who entered the job market with high aspirations, the new environment has become a nightmare. There is no incentive for them to perform, since performance is no longer a measurement of success or used to gauge reward. Today many managers find themselves in positions where they have plateaued. With no prospect of upward mobility, often it also means no more increases in pay. The old pay-and-hierarchy system no longer protects these managers and today it is more likely that these managers will find themselves in situations where a pay cut is more likely than a pay increase.

What happened to respect, dignity and credibility?

When downsizing takes place, management frequently fails to recognize the impact on people. Although corporations provide severance packages and other services such as outplacement counseling, many corporations fail to fully understand how to treat employees who are laid off and those who are still working for them. During the process of employee layoffs, the methodology used by corporations is often one devoid of any respect for the employee as a person.

There are many instances when corporations have gone into a downsizing mode, where employees laid off have been escorted off the premises by security guards. Downsized managers, once the leaders of the organization, have found their offices under lock and key and summarily dispatched out of the building. This type of corporate behavior is not only distasteful, but shows no respect for employees who most probably have served the company for a number of years under the belief that management respected them. Escorted like a thief by security guards the laid off employees have no dignity left, their only redemption is the lack of handcuffs.

As the downsized employee is locked out of his or her office and escorted out of the premises, another factor has been overlooked. What of the feelings of the employees who are left behind? When and where corporations have used these tactics, it has left no doubt in the mind of survivors that credibility in management is probably non-existent. Employees do not forget these actions, and will operate knowing it could happen to them next. The negative effect on corporate culture is inevitable. All the future exhortations by management will almost certainly fall on deaf ears. No matter how reassuring management will try to be in its future pronouncements, it is unlikely that employees will find it credible. When management does not treat its workers with respect and dignity, how can they expect to be credible when they talk about values and corporate goals?

Management and Leadership

Leaders are supposed to create corporate vision and shape corporate values but in this era of downsizing it is becoming extremely difficult for leaders to work effectively because they have lost credibility. Workers no longer believe their leaders as an air of cynicism has gradually crept into the corporate environment. This has come about as corporate leadership has ignored the human factor in shifting its attention to the bottom line. Short-term policies designed to satisfy the shareholders have blurred the vision of corporate leaders. Management often ignores the fact that a company may no longer be competitive because its strategic plans no longer fit the changing environment. Their actions and policies have been to increase earnings per share to the detriment of their employees, since it is easier to cut payroll and benefit costs than to make changes to other corporate policies. It is a quick fix remedy, which does not address the real issues of planning, research and development and productivity.

While downsizing activities are taking place to reduce payroll costs, these same executives increase their compensation as many corporate leaders fail to practice what they preach. As a result in many organizations today often the pronounced values conflict with the practiced values. Many leaders "talk the talk" but very few actually "walk the talk". While they say something to get their employees' attention and help them achieve a new corporate goal, their next step is to prescribe another round of layoffs to offset the increased costs necessary to implement their new strategy.

No wonder there is little trust left in the corporate environment. There exists an increased cynicism in our work environment as Kouzes and Posner write:

> "Substantially fewer of us believe that the leaders and managers of our business and governmental institutions are capable enough or trustworthy enough to guide us to the top in this intensely competitive global market place. There is a growing sense among employees that management is not competent to handle these tough challenges, that they are not quite telling us the truth, and that they are motivated more by greed than by concern for the customer, the employee, or the country." [3]

Very often these decisions are taken in the 'mahogany suites' of the corporation with little input from the lower echelons of the corporation. Of course, workers view these decisions as authoritarian and dictatorial and feel very isolated. In December 1989, *Fortune* magazine used the phrase *trust gap* to define employee-management relations. As a result of a decade of reengineering and downsizing, the gap is more likely to be a *chasm* that unfortunately is not going to be bridged soon.

Thus far our whole discussion has been on the factors and reasons for change. To be ready to start a new building, an appropriate site and foundation are required. The ravages of past change methodologies demand that we examine all the past circumstances in order to prevent the same mistakes to be repeated in our reconstruction task. If this is the result of our past failures, we are bound to repeat the same mistakes if we do not have a plan of action to correct the present situation and avoid historical mistakes. To proceed on the right track we must ask ourselves the question . . .

Part Two

THE BUILDING

CHAPTER 5

What's next?

"To see what is in front of one's nose requires a constant struggle."
– George Orwell.

"If you don't create change now . . . you may not be around
to tell the story."
– Unknown.

THE DISCUSSION IN previous chapters has given us an idea about the reasons for the changes in our work environment. Each of the factors reviewed has had an impact on how work has been restructured and why the lack of trust that exists in the corporate world has occurred. As the forces of globalization, technology and workers' needs change, it is imperative that we find alternatives to our current and traditional concepts about work. Jeremy Rifkin, an economist and author of *The End of Work: Technology, Jobs and Your Future* believes that technological change is not likely to bring forth increases in the number of jobs, but instead – as industrialized countries become more technical – human labor has been supplanted by devices. However, this is only one man's point of view, there are others who believe that employment will increase as a result of new technology, not in traditional areas, but in industries which have not even been thought of today. Quite correctly the proponents of this theory use the

Internet as an example of technology helping to create new industries and new jobs. The question is: Are we prepared for this shift from traditional jobs to the new information age jobs?

Earlier we examined the factors and consequences of change. Now it is time for us to have a good look at a new environment, which will address the issues facing work, as it will likely be in the next millennium. We must take into consideration that wants and needs have changed, that stress is a part of our daily life and may be the cause of many of our social problems. The 'them and us' attitude that prevails between workers and management must be altered. A totally different approach must be found to alleviate the socio-economic problems that accompany the end of work as we have seen in the latter years of the nineties. We must learn from our past mistakes and anticipate the trends, which will affect us. Most of all, we must learn to adapt in order to survive in the new millennium. The effects of change are too rapid and too encompassing for us to maintain the *status quo*. To do so could well result in stagnation and chaos. Leaders must use their competencies to forge a new environment, which will address the existing and emerging problems. Individuals must learn to adapt to the new circumstances. In the work environment, workers must understand that the 'old contract' of employment is no longer valid or operational. A new system must be put into place to avoid the problems, which have and are plaguing society in the latter part of the twentieth century. A new era is just beginning. What we need to find are new solutions to existing and new problems. In order to make changes to our current work environment, we shall examine the current trends, requirements, and adaptations forced upon us by change. Each of the factors discussed below will elicit questions about the future of work and the work environment and at the end of the chapter I will prescribe a possible solution to these thorny problems that both workers and organizations will face in future.

Technology

The speed at which technology changes our lives is now so rapid that people and organizations have problems adjusting. However, as we move along this path the acceleration becomes even more pronounced. The effects are not only found in the level of unemployment, but also in the ways we work. There are advantages to the increase in technology, and we must recognize them in order to rectify the current problems.

As the 'information highway' grows, people are increasingly able to work from home. The barriers to communication fall and enable better transfer of data. For example the Nasdaq exchange operates 24hrs a day. Many North American firms use computer labor from India to do work for them. When America shuts down for the day, India is starting the workday, so by transferring work between staff in India and America the work is done on a 24-hour basis.

The physical location of work has become irrelevant in a certain sense. As data becomes easily transferable people can telecommute – that is, perform work from home or satellite offices and transmit their work to their employer's office base. This will impact on the size of offices and their location, while transportation woes in big cities may be lessened. Will we still require the big tower offices? Maybe not! What will we do with those expensive office buildings in our major cities? Will the solution be to transform them into work/residence accommodation?

Employment

The result of the reengineering craze of the eighties and nineties has left workers wary of their future. Workers who are still employed by 'restructured organizations' find themselves working longer hours and performing more tasks to fill the gap left by their laid off colleagues. Since the long-term safety net of job security no longer exists, workers are considering an alternative to the old daily grind of working in an office for somebody on a regular basis. The needs of workers have changed. For some, quality of life is becoming a major factor in the way they want to mix work and family activities. Many workers cannot find full time positions and have reluctantly opted to work part-time. Some have two or three part-time jobs these days, having to carefully balance their work life with their social life and match them with their economic resources.

Today's workers are likely to be better educated and desire a greater say in the decision making process. Many knowledge workers do not want to work in large bureaucratic structures anymore. Since loyalty is a dying attribute, workers are more likely to change jobs whenever an opportunity arises. Corporations will find themselves at a loss to retain workers and the costs of recruiting and training will rise accordingly.

The past actions of management have produced a new breed of employee – the mercenary. This new worker offers his/her services under contract, instead of being an employee of the organization. The mercenary is independent in thinking and has no specific allegiances. The major criteria are to offer their skills and competencies to an organization and move on when the task is finished. In this new environment, how do we match the workers needs with those of the organization? How do we create an environment, which both serves the worker and the organization and fulfill their mutual goals?

Needs

As we saw above, the needs of both employees and employers are changing. While organizations have to become more competitive and more customer focused, employees on the other hand want to satisfy their needs for recognition and reward for a job well done. The aftermath of the restructuring of corporations has also taught workers that in the eyes of the corporation, employees are **not** number one, and that they must look after themselves. Their needs are no longer just monetary. Workers today want respect to go with their employment. Their self-esteem has been battered over the past decade and they want to recover their dignity. Workers want to participate and be given information that enables them to contribute to the success of the organization. Rhetoric does not cut the mustard anymore. The knowledge worker is more informed and does not accept management's pronouncements as fact. They no longer want to be viewed as the problem but rather as part of the solution.

Can the needs of workers and corporations be equally fulfilled? How do we bring the two sides together to solve problems and attain their mutual objectives? What role do unions and governments play to resolve this issue?

Stress

As a result of the past actions of corporations during the restructuring and reengineering phases, workers have been put under enormous stress. Studies show this is not true of workers who were at the wrong end of the downsizing policies but those who remained as well.

Those employees who were unfortunate to be laid off during a corporate downsizing effort have the stress of finding a new job. In difficult economic times it is increasingly more difficult to find a job which will provide the same economic benefits as the old one. In many cases the older employee, in the 45 to 55 year range finds it virtually impossible to find a new job. They quickly resort to using their severance package and then their savings and after that they sometimes fall back on social security. The stress to the laid off employee is not only personal – in many cases it may also be transferred to other members of the family.

Workers who are still employed are hardly immune to stress. The departure of their former colleagues has saddled them with longer working hours and more responsibilities, often coupled with the same pay. The fear of being laid off in the next round of corporate restructuring does not disappear; in fact it contributes to further anxiety. Workers are given more responsibilities but they are rarely given more control. The stress factor puts pressure on employees' health and wellness, and corporations start losing productivity. Under these circumstances, if management's reasons for restructuring were increased productivity, the result may be the total opposite. Productivity instead of increasing takes a retrograde step.

However Gene Kopetz (1997) for *Business Week* reports that, a study of the 10 largest downsizers in the 1990-1995 period, done by economist Michael Cox and Richard Alin showed the opposite. He points out:

> "Altogether the group jettisoned almost 850,000 workers over that period, they report. And the group's collective output – measured by inflation-adjusted sales – declined by nearly 10%. But the key point is that as the 10 companies shed some 29% of their workers, productivity or output (real sales) per worker rose by nearly 28% or 5.6% per year. That compares with an1 annual per-worker productivity gain of 1.5% for the economy as a whole."[1]

This apparent paradox is a problematic issue. If productivity gains are being achieved through downsizing what will corporations do? Will they continue the trend to become more competitive? What does this mean for the future of work and the employee? Will stress related problems continue to grow and affect the social fabric?

Compensation

Downsizing in the past decade has been used to reduce the size of the payroll. Unfortunately, in so doing, corporations in some cases got rid of the wrong people. Often the people targeted for layoffs were the ones whose performance was deemed inadequate by management. In some instances however, managers were let go because it was simply cheaper to give them a lump-sum severance package than keep them on the payroll with a high salary. In these cases, managers were chosen not because of their performance but strictly to reduce the payroll costs. Another instance is the voluntary retirement policies of downsizing. In these cases a number of very good and bright employees took the offer and left the corporation. These employees were perhaps the risk takers of the firm and they left because they had no fear of the future. The loss to the corporation was more than just financial! The firm lost expertise it had paid over the years and to replace it the firm will incur additional training and recruiting costs in the future.

In the mean time, the compensation packages of executives got more lucrative. Performance-related pay at the senior levels is quite common now. However, when it comes to 'non-performance' we rarely hear of cut backs for executives. While they receive enormous rewards when the company does well, they rarely lose these rewards in proportion to any losses when they occur. This state of affairs cannot be conducive to good management/employee relationships and can be the root cause of many labor relations problems with unions.

Can businesses and corporations continue on this path of destruction through compensation? Can the gap between workers' and executives' rewards continue? What are the answers to equitable performance related pay?

Them v/s Us

As we move towards a new type of organization we must also look positively at the end of some of the old expectations and face the new realities of this new work environment. For middle managers and workers alike, the old expectations of job security and employment with one firm for life are gone forever. The new realities are that all of us must face a future that will see our working life made up of several careers. Workers will have to constantly upgrade their skills to make themselves more employable.

In this new scenario both management and workers will have to work together to address these issues. Management has to bring all employees into the loop. Strategic decisions can no longer be made without effective communication with the stakeholders. The careers of workers, especially middle managers, will have to be structured differently. It is incumbent upon management to provide a meaningful role for displaced middle managers. As their careers reach a plateau or the establishment of work teams takes the place of hierarchical structures, middle managers will have to be treated with dignity and compassion. They must be given the opportunity to contribute and maintain their self-respect. The 'them and us' attitude of the past must give way to more participation and meaningful communication.

How does management face these issues? What types of structures best suit a participative work environment? How do organizations replace rhetoric with straight talk?

Part-time/ Full-time Workers

Workers would rather work part-time than not at all. In some cases workers would like to work part-time to balance their family commitments with work. It is incumbent upon organizations to take these factors into account and provide for work sharing and flextime. Workers who no longer work full-time can well serve the organization of tomorrow. The advances of the information highway will provide the worker with the ability to telecommute instead of using conventional means of transportation.

The practice of not providing benefits for part-time workers will have to change, as is already the case with certain organizations. A re-thinking about cost cutting and balancing corporate and workers' needs must take place very quickly in the face of a changing work environment which no longer operates under the same parameters of the post World War II era.

What steps have to be taken to promote part-time work? Is it beneficial for organizations to provide benefits to part-time workers? How does technology help the blending of part-time and full-time staff?

Globalization

As more countries deregulate access to their markets, the effect of globalization will expand. In the past, countries took a very protectionist attitude towards their domestic markets. With the establishment of the new trade agreements, market barriers are gradually falling. India, and China for example, which once had some of the most protective domestic markets in the world, are opening their trade frontiers, which will result in increasing trade in these part of the world. Due to competition, other new territories like Indonesia will likely follow. The resulting effect will be a gradual increase in the shifting of jobs and activities from industrialized countries to developing countries as corporations seek competitiveness, especially where lower labor costs exist. Proximity to the market place will also be a very important factor and manufacturing will shift to places closer to the point of sale.

As corporations move their activities to developing countries, there seems to be an increasing trend to the use of locals instead of expatriates to manage the company's foreign activities. The consequences of this policy will have an impact on the recruitment and training of future staff. The sensibilities of local culture will become a very important factor in searching for executives with the right competencies for positions in multi-nationals. An understanding of corporate culture alone will not be a sufficient criterion for success. Competencies will have to include an affinity and appreciation for foreign cultures and understanding of the cultures of diverse and ethnic personnel. As the number of women and ethnic workers in corporations grow, managing a diverse workforce will become extremely important.

How do these factors, which have an impact on human resources management, impact the policies of corporations? How do we recruit personnel with the right competencies to operate in a diverse environment? How do we restructure with empathy as corporations go international or global? What role does government and unions play in this continuing movement towards increase competitiveness around the world?

The Troika

In redefining the way we look at work the role of the three most important players must be improved. In the past, although governments, unions and corporations have worked together to solve problems, in many cases it has worked well, but in some cases agreements between these parties have caused enormous damage in one way or another. As a result the role of each one of these institutions must be scrutinized, because any attempt to change the work environment will greatly depend on the actions and behavior of leaders from these three groups. We can call these three institutions the 'troika' because there are so linked to one another that decisions made by one always affects the others. This truism requires further elaboration. Let me explain.

When corporations and unions enter into negotiations about work conditions and compensation, their agreement has an important effect on each other – and on government. If the agreement, for example, results in layoffs the government is affected because it is the administrator of employment insurance. When government policies affect the profitability or operations of corporations, workers are affected as corporations adjust to implement these policies. Unions get involved at one stage or another to protect their members.

Depending on the political leanings and receptivity of the existing government, pressures from unions can affect government policies. In the case of a left-leaning governments, like President Obama's, who are generally supported by unions, policies will tend to be more labor friendly. Legislation favoring higher taxes, more social benefits and work related regulations are more likely to be passed by such a government. The implementation of such policies may have economic effects such as higher inflation, increasing debt and a decline in competitiveness due to a higher wage, benefit and regulatory cost component of products. As a result, corporations may react by moving production abroad to areas where such costs are lower. In turn, they may close factories, lay off domestic workers, which may affect entire communities and perhaps regions.

On the other hand, a right-leaning government may promote policies that are more favorable to the business community. In this case, policies such as reduced taxation, deregulation of industries and decrease in social benefits are more likely to be adopted. While a reduction in taxation may bring forth an increase in consumer spending, these policies may also result in higher inflation. To balance the reduction in taxation, governments may either cut back on social services, or they may choose not to cut back but print money instead, resulting in increasing debt. Deregulation may bring in foreign competition, which in the short term is beneficial to the consumer, but it may in the longer term cause a rationalization of the industry, resulting in bankruptcies and layoffs.

During good economic times, we may see increased labor unrest, as unions position themselves to make gains for their members. Recent examples include the 'Occupy Wall street' and repeated demonstrations, at almost all World Conferences. In some cases, notwithstanding the other economic factors, which may exist at the time, unions will press for changes in their collective agreement based on profits made by corporations. Since it is customary for unions to levy membership fees as a percentage of members' wages, it is in the interest of the unions to force corporations to negotiate into agreements which provides for a greater number of employees, thus making gains in both membership numbers and increased financial base.

As we can see, these three players are undeniably linked to each other. Their decisions can have severe implications on the economy, employer/employee relations and social and community issues to name but a few. It is therefore imperative for us to find a way for these players to work closer together to make decisions not based on partisan or/and political reasons. As already mentioned the effects are far too damaging for decisions to be made in isolation. In most industrialized countries, earlier economic decisions of government have caused the accumulation of large debts. Unions have acquired wage gains and other worker benefits, which have made many corporations less competitive. Corporations have reacted to the forces of competition from emerging and developing countries by moving their operations to cheaper locations. They have downsized and reduced their labor force to reduce their costs, creating and in some cases, the collapse of work as we know it.

Do we continue on this path of self-destruction? How do we work together to solve the problems, which face workers in most industrialized countries? Do we, in certain circumstances, keep current legislation that gives unions so much power? What about the right to work? This relationship between government, corporations and unions will be discussed in greater detail in Chapter 16, where we shall look at the role of each member of the troika, and offer alternatives to current philosophies.

Flatter organizations

As organizations downsized and restructured themselves, many started to use the concept of teamwork as a means to flatten the pyramids of most large organizations. The idea is to get rid of the generally unneeded echelons of control and by so doing eliminate many middle management positions. At the heart of this concept was the idea of using teams to make the organization more flexible and more competitive. Instead of the multi-level organizations of yesterday, many corporations are adopting the use of multi-disciplined teams either on permanent basis or based on project-by-project needs. The flexibility and the ability for workers to move from one project to another project create an environment where promotion up the ladder is no longer the only way to achieve success. It has been found that team members work more harmoniously together and in this environment, the productivity and creativity of workers is often on a high.

There are merits to the team concept, because as we flatten organizations we supposedly get decision making closer to the people who implement and actually do the work. However, there are already cracks showing within some organizations that have used the team concept. Once again the workload and the decision-making have been passed down to a new level, but in many cases, the rhetoric continues. Teams are put into place but true empowerment still may not exist in all cases. People are given more work and responsibility but it is often accompanied by a lack of authority, little recognition and proper rewards. The misuse of this concept may continue the trend of cost cutting without too much regard to the human assets of the organization.

Reward systems have changed somewhat, but in many cases they still remain the same. Few organizations have completely embraced peer reviews and performance-related pay systems. In unionized organizations it has been extremely difficult to amend the old collective agreements to encompass a better and equitable reward-based system. Unions still argue for higher wages based on cost-of living indices that are often gained without higher productivity. As soon as a recession or economic downturn is over, unions start making demands for higher wages, which can result in a possible round of layoffs by management to avoid increased costs.

All is not negative, however. There are corporations, which have instituted teams very well and are benefiting from the newly found enthusiasm of their workers. Stock options and bonuses are frequently part of the reward system instituted in these organizations. Instead of immediate supervisors, peers, internal and external customers perform performance reviews. Bonuses, in these cases, are frequently awarded to the team as a whole instead of individuals.

How do companies gain the full benefit of teams? What steps do they put into place to maintain cohesion and participation? How do they get rid of management rhetoric? *(See Chapter 15)*

Participative Management

Together we have examined the different forces and factors, which have caused such havoc within the work environment in the eighties and nineties. I have asked many questions about the existing concepts surrounding the decision making process. I have reviewed the roles and actions of governments, corporations and unions. It is time to provide some solutions. They may not be the panacea awaited by workers and society, but they will at least provide a basis for a change in our current beliefs associated with employment and the roles of workers within corporations, and society as a whole.

To begin with an atmosphere of collaboration is an essential start to alleviate our current problems. Business must promote an environment where employees are treated as assets, not liabilities who will be discarded at the drop of a hat. Participation of the stakeholders in the decision making process is also crucial, in all areas of society – in government, in corporations and unionized environments. This shift must take place. It can be achieved through a new type of leadership, one that fosters empowerment of all stakeholders. Leaders must become trustworthy and lead by 'walking the talk'. Rhetoric is no longer acceptable.

Organizations must learn from their past mistakes, anticipate future problems and adapt in order to survive and rejuvenate the work environment.

To halt the havoc caused through restructuring and downsizing, I advocate a new type of leadership more focused on participative management and collaboration among all players – government, corporations, employees and unions.

Some of our corporate leaders have failed to demonstrate a willingness to change their policies, and have continued to work in isolation while asking workers for more cooperation and a greater contribution to the bottom line. How do the leaders of tomorrow's corporations expect to gain cooperation if they continue to manage in the old fashioned way, the autocratic way? This issue is so fundamental to the success of future work environment that we must discuss the different characteristics of good . . .

CHAPTER 6

Leadership

"The new leader is clearly distinguished from the old-style boss.
A boss creates fear – a leader confidence,
A boss fixes blame – a leader corrects mistakes."
– Russell Ewing.

THE SUCCESS OF any organization is largely dependent upon the quality of its leadership. As we discuss the fate of the future corporation it is important to look at the issues of leadership and the characteristics and competencies required of future leaders. Mary and Dean Tjosvold's definition of leadership state:

"Leadership is a special and noble but also very human and knowable. It is based on fundamental values of respect, caring, and achievement. Leaders reach out and inspire people to fulfill their potentials. They bring us together to find out our common ground and accomplish our shared aspirations."

In the past, great leaders have been associated with terms, which sometimes have not been very complimentary to them. While words such as autocratic, dictatorial and barbaric have been commonly used to describe some leaders, other words such as charismatic, kind, and visionary have been used to describe other leading figures.

Although different types, characteristics and descriptions have been attributed to different leaders, it is also true that most of them share a common thread: they all are change agents. Mary and Dean Tjosvold also wrote:

> "Leaders recognize that the status quo is an illusion, that change is relentless, and that organizations must adapt if they are to survive and flourish." [2]

All leaders have been instrumental in effecting change in one way or another. The change does not occur in the political arena, the community, the corporate world and even lesser areas of day-to-day life without a catalyst. In all cases the people we commonly call leaders have been instrumental in altering the course of events in one way or another for the better and in some cases for worse. Similarly some, by taking no action still affected the outcome of certain issues.

Where the change effected has been successful, we have showered these leaders with praise. Conversely when things have gone sour, history has remembered these leaders with many unkind words. There is a bright and dark side to leadership and we must recognize that fact early in our discussion. These two sides affect the characteristics displayed by many leaders, and they also determine their style during their course of action. For example, an autocratic leader may display a bullying and controlling attitude, while a compassionate leader may display a more conciliatory approach to solving solutions. Recent research on leadership has also shown that males and females do have different styles of leadership. Since the number of women involved in decision-making is increasing, it is only fitting that we also contrast these styles.

Before we discuss the characteristics of leaders we should look at some other common issues that may influence the action and behavior of leaders. In the first instance, we must acknowledge that three distinct areas of leadership affect our lives and each of these actions has a significant impact on our daily lives. Here I refer reference is to the corporate, political and unionized environment. We cannot have a discussion on leadership without addressing the influence of these three areas just mentioned. We must also understand some of the theories of managerial economics pertaining to the firm in order to understand the motivation of modern management and its leaders. Let us look at these areas of influence.

Leadership Arenas

As mentioned earlier, there are three major arenas where leadership exerts itself and plays a major role in our daily life. They are the political, the labor movement (unions) and the corporate. These three arenas have a somewhat symbiotic relationship. They depend on each other in one way or another and they work together or against each other to achieve their respective goals and objectives. Their actions and decisions have a major impact on the future of the economy, the corporate environment and peoples' lives in general. For these reasons it is important to examine the leadership and motives of leaders in these three arenas, and we must understand their motivation in order to shape the participative working environment of the next millennium.

Political

When we speak of leaders, although persons from different fields of endeavor are mentioned, very often the first names that spring to mind are those of political or military leaders. These leaders have either left a mark on society or are in the process of doing something, which will affect our lives. In the political arena leaders are often motivated by an ideology as they tackle and solve issues based on their political beliefs. Ideology is very instrumental in the shaping of policies and the resolution of crises. Political leaders based on their political leanings address economic crises and therefore political decisions have an enormous effect on future corporate and union decisions. It is important to understand the ideological leanings of political leaders in order to understand their motives. Leaders in the political arena are not only motivated by their beliefs, but are also influenced by the anticipated effect of their decisions on the popular vote except of course in a dictatorship.

Unions

Workers' unions were formed to protect the rights of workers, and today the movement has grown to include collective bargaining and a number of issues, which were not thought of at its inception. Today unions have gained enormous power through the size of their membership and the ability to bring activities to a standstill through strike actions. Union leaders have become skillful negotiators who influence both political and corporate decisions. In many instances legislation gives certain rights to unions to levy dues out of their members' wages, which is their main source of revenue. These revenues are sometimes used to finance strikes. In effect, it is in unions' best interest to raise the earnings of their members to increase their revenue base. Could this contribute to problems in future negotiations between management and unions?

Unions' actions and motivations affect thousands if not millions of workers in the industrialized world. Their negotiation strategies are more sophisticated than they used to be and have great influence on their members, the public and corporate policies. The collective bargaining process is not confined to just wages, but includes job security, benefits, training, safety and other issues. Each agreement between unions and corporations usually increases the costs to the corporation. Where these costs are too high, very often the compromise is to settle for a reduction in staff. In these instances many workers, often members of unions, find themselves affected by downsizing. If management and the union do not agree, the alternative often results in corporate relocation and even closure of the company.

Corporate

Leaders in the corporate world are usually chosen for their competencies, based on academic, previous track record and technical abilities that can better serve the respective corporation. It is hoped they shape the corporation in such a way as to make them successful and profitable for the owners. Often their motivation is based on monetary reward based and in some cases by their own personal goals. These people make decisions, which affect people on a large or a small scale depending on the size of the corporation they lead. Where the corporation is in the multinational league, corporate decisions can also affect the political and economical environment. Many multinationals, such as General Motors, Apple and Microsoft have budgets, which dwarf some third world countries' national budgets. In these cases, corporate leaders have become extremely powerful and are responsible for more than their immediate employees. For example, the decision to build or to close a factory will have economic impacts on the immediate community where the factory is located. Similarly, while the transfer of manufacturing facilities to third world countries will result in economic woes in the industrialized world, it provides growth in the emerging economies. In the recent past decisions of corporate leaders, especially those of large multinationals, have not only impacted their immediate organizations, but have also had repercussions on local politics and industrial relations. The monetary rewards of corporate leaders may not yet be a political issue in most industrialized countries, but it is certainly becoming a source of conflict between management, unions, and some stockholders. Corporate downsizing decisions to benefit the bottom line are another source of conflict with unions. This can be an uncomfortable problem for politicians who promise their constituents more or better jobs to gain their votes at the polling booths.

There is a broad understanding that corporate leadership is primarily responsible to run a firm for a profit. However, in the marketplace, the operations of a corporation do not exactly match the demands of society for goods and services. The firm must make decisions, sometimes without all the available information, and it therefore requires planning and strategies to survive in the face of risk and adversity. History has demonstrated that in a competitive environment private firms are more efficient and effective in allocating scarce resources. This is why many governments are deregulating and privatizing some industries.

The Firm and it's behavior

In order to better understand the workings of corporations and specifically their leaders we should take a brief and simple look at the common models of managerial economics.

The Profit-Maximization Model: from this point of view, the assumption is that the main objective of an organization is to maximize the benefits, products and services provided by the firm's operations in relation to its costs. The results sought after are profits.

The Sales-Maximization Model: is the alternative to the profit-maximization model. It is based in the belief that a firm should have a certain level of profit, but that short-term profits can also be sacrificed to secure a better competitive position, which will result in more profits in the long run.

The Growth-Maximization Model: here, growth and growth potential are usually the yardstick by which corporate success is measured, and it usually depends on the continued availability of large profit streams. In effect a decision to maximize growth is a decision to maximize profits in the long run.

The Managerial-Behavior Models: These models deal with the relationships between managers and shareholders in publicly held firms:

The Managerial-Utility Model: assumes that the owners' and stockholders' priority is to maximize profits, while managers have a priority to satisfy their needs and desires, often motivated by their salaries and benefits. However, empirical evidence has shown that managers have a personal motive to maximize profits, especially today where executives' compensation is often linked to stock options.

The Managerial-Discretion Model: purports that managers are free to pursue their own interests, as long as they have satisfied the needs for a certain level of profit which will provide for a satisfactory dividend to shareholders and enough for future growth. In this case it is assumed that the manager's self-interest lies in other things besides salary. These interests may include perquisites, such as a limousine and other expenses, and sometimes the number and the type of people supervised. It is believed that managers operating under this model spend more on staff than those operating under a profit-maximization model. However, empirical evidence is only mildly supportive of this model.

The Agency Model: concerns itself with the contractual relationship between the stockholders and managers. This model usually favors incentives such as bonuses and stock options as a motivator for executives to maximize the owners' wealth, although in many cases it does not guarantee peak performance.

The Value-Added Maximization Model (Japanese Model): While most western firms concentrate on short-run profits, and earnings-per-share in the short-run, Japanese firms use a short-run approach as a guide to manage the firm, and attempt to maximize the value-added of the productive activities. This model is a long-range concept, which attempts to maximize the benefits of management, employees, suppliers and shareholders, and therefore tends to foster participative actions within the firm.

The above models have been described in order to provide some rational explanation for the behavior of management and the consequences resulting from their actions. In my further examination of participative management I shall refer to one or more of these models to illustrate the pros and cons of the current management style that prevails in western organizations. At this stage why don't you consider the following: What model is your company? What do you like or don't like about it?

Characteristics of Leaders

All leaders share a number of common characteristics. Some leaders may have all of them, some may be deficient in some areas but there is a distinct general understanding that to be a leader one must demonstrate some, if not all, of these characteristics to be successful. Their importance may vary with the circumstances or environment but they are important enough for us to discuss them. In my proposal for a participative management model, these characteristics will play an important role in shaping the appropriate culture for its success. As more women enter the upper echelons of management, it is becoming quite apparent that the genders can differ in styles and approach, and in observance of this reality I shall also discuss the differences in traits and characteristics of male and female leaders. To begin with let us examine the traits that are more commonly used to describe leaders.

Courage

Difficult problems require difficult decisions. As a result successful leaders are often recognized for their courage. They usually display enormous strength in the face of adversity, concerned with solving the immediate problem. Their risk-taking nature makes them fearless of the unknown and failure is not a word that slows them down. Often they are the first one to jump into the fray and lead by example. Richard Branson of Virgin Corporation is an example of a risk taker and a courageous leader. He quit school at sixteen to run a magazine. Today, from time to time he will undertake long distance hot-air balloon expeditions to fulfill his risk-taking disposition. As a risk taker, he also encourages his followers to take risks.

Leaders do not see failure as a catastrophe, but rather as a learning process, which provides a lesson for the future. However this willingness to stand, above the crowd, may some time leave them vulnerable.

Focused

Leaders are focused. They are often drawn to a task to the point of obsession. They approach problems with a single-mindedness that is not found in many people. Once they have defined their vision they are committed to it. This unwavering attitude helps them to maintain the relationship between members of a group.

Visionary

It is often said that leaders have a vision, one which is usually long term and futuristic by most standards. They have the ability to see what has to be done and how it should be done. As E. Wille and P. Hodgson wrote:

> "A prime task of the top leadership of an organization is to give the grand vision of the future. People at all levels can then break down this vision to arrive at their piece of the big picture." [3]

Their vision of an event or accomplishment is clear to them, although it may be fuzzy to others. Armed with this ability to foresee, the leader is able to provide a clear goal and direction for others to follow. Great leaders with vision are those who have been able to galvanize their followers' attention with some utopian or inspirational ideology, design and direction.

By the way not all leaders' so called visions have necessarily led to success. History has also provided us with some examples of catastrophic ends of followers and leaders alike. For example Adolf Hitler got people to follow him, however the results for society were catastrophic.

Messenger

As visionaries, leaders often have a message meant to articulate an ideology. The message is usually simple and often uses imagery to illustrate their thoughts. Through simple language they can reach large numbers of people and sell them the message. They can effectively promote change because they understand and know that the messenger is often more important than the message.

Communicator

In order to get their message across great leaders are usually great communicators. Not only do they deliver a simple message they listen. They draw energy from their followers and adapt their thoughts to maximize the effect of the message.

Timely

Circumstances and events often dictate the success of leaders, and indeed most leaders have an inexplicable sense of timing. They seem to be at the right place at the right time. Some create the circumstances and even crises to suit their timing.

Decisive

Because leaders are viewed as 'doers' instead of just thinkers, they are usually very decisive in their approach to problems. They excel in moments of crisis, whether created by themselves or by others. Under pressure they perform with great speed and decisiveness, giving the impression that nothing can stop them. This ability to be quick and clear in making decisions is at the heart of their success. Mere mortals usually are slow to react and make a rational decision. Leaders react quickly and provide an answer, perhaps not always the best, but they are usually able to break the *status quo* and move on to the next problem and solution.

Charismatic

Some leaders have enormous charisma, which they use to convey their captivating message and enhance their communication. Charisma is often said to be a gift. However, in most cases it not a personal trait but rather a characteristic bestowed upon or attributed to leaders by their followers. Lewis Losoncy writes:

> "Ironically, leaders are the most dependent people in the organization. The higher one is the more people he or she needs to hold them up." [4]

Often "followers" are willing to forgo some of their individualism to follow their leader. Through this transfer of power leaders can mesmerize their followers to the point of stupidity. Those leaders, who have a darker side, have even sometimes driven their followers to death. The charismatic effect of a leader cannot be separated from the willingness of followers who are actually projecting their abilities and qualities onto the leader, and by so doing, to virtually submit to a fate, which is outside of their control.

Credible

Because leaders' behaviors tend to be consistent with their pronouncements and beliefs, they are usually credible. Kouzes and Posner wrote:

> "What the leader does is the single most important factor in demonstrating to others what is acceptable – and unacceptable – behavior in our organizations. Effectively the leader's behavior is the model we use to determine or calibrate our own behavior and choices." [4]

Credibility is the characteristic that gives leaders the ability to establish and assert authority over people and situations. This authority however is not used to dominate but rather to draw from followers and captivate their attention for the immediate task at hand. In empowering and mobilizing peoples' ideas to achieve their goals, something very important happens; leaders gain more respectability and credibility. They gain in stature because they consistently do what they say they will do. In other words they always 'walk the talk'.

Trusted

Last but not least of these sought after characteristics is trust. Good leaders gain their followers' trust. They earn that trust by their consistent actions. Good leaders delegate and empower because they trust their followers' abilities, and use their acquired respect to motivate instead of dominate their subordinates. Leaders are trusted because they take responsibility for their actions as well as the actions of their subordinates. They support their followers and gain support in return. This trust is further used to provide an 'open-door' policy which makes leaders approachable. Through this trust they create better communication and openness, which promotes participation, creativity and innovation.

Gender Leadership

Although more women are entering the workforce, the proportion of females in the corporate boardrooms is not increasing. Due to circumstances more traditional than factual, males have dominated the higher echelons of corporations. Males control the majority of executive positions and are therefore, in control of the decision-making process. Hence leadership has been viewed as a male dominated bastion and very few women have been able to break this archaic tradition. However, in politics, more than in the corporate world, this situation is changing. Many world leaders of the post World War II era have been women, Margaret Thatcher, Golda Meir and Indira Gandhi are but a few women who have been successful as world leaders and have made an impact on our lives.

Recent research has focused on the male/female leadership style and the left/right brain correlation. In the 'behavioral' approach, research on leadership has been undertaken for different types of groups, ranging from boardrooms, boy scouts movement, etc., in order to identify the aspects of leadership. Results from different researchers have narrowed the discussion to two fundamental aspects. One, that leaders focus on the "immediate task" undertaken by the group, and two, that leaders focus on the maintenance of "relationships" between members of the group. For the purposes of a participative style of management I believe that it is appropriate to provide some background to examine this issue.

Male Leadership

At the risk of offending a number of my readers, it must be said that traditionally leadership has been viewed as a male domain. In most cultures the male has been seen as the dominating gender, generally responsible as the protector and food provider for the family. Based on this traditional point of view it is clear why males have been the leaders of most types of organizations. However, there are other factors at play. Recently behavioral research has concluded that men tend to use the (logical) left side of their brain. It is also known that the left side of the brain relates to areas such as spatial relationships and analytical skills. As mentioned before, one of the aspects of leadership focuses on the ability to finish a task. These two male characteristics go hand in hand. Most corporations focus on the task of making a profit, and men with their left-side orientation do well at achieving this goal. Similarly financial analysis and engineering skills are more in tune with the left side of the brain. It is therefore, natural for male leaders to do well in organizations, which are task oriented, and where analytical skills are required. This may be one of the reasons why males often are corporate leaders.

Female Leadership

To contrast the male characteristics stated above, we cannot ignore the special skills that women bring to fore. Women have been extremely good in roles as political leaders, but proportionately very few have been great corporate leaders. Not because they have failed in the corporate arena, but rather because very few of them have had the opportunity to prove themselves as corporate leaders. The female role in society has traditionally been more oriented towards inter-personal relationships, getting members of the family to work together. Female leadership tends to be more conservative, and is preoccupied with the maintenance of the social environment. This is very much in keeping with the results of behavioral researchers who have found that females predominantly use the (emotional) right side of their brain. This right brain predominance makes females more skillful communicators, more intuitive and also emotional. In addition women can be very creative and good negotiators. These skills are of course better suited for politics and organizations where the leadership aspect of 'relationship maintenance' is required. Two examples of resounding success, in addition to the other women mentioned earlier come to mind. The first being the case of Marilyn Carlson Nelson, CEO of Carlson Companies, one of the largest travel service companies in the world. Although at first, not fully endorsed by her father for succession as the Chief Executive, she has proved to be very successful in the expansion and growth of the company, whose success is based on respects for relationships, and the establishment and maintenance of loyalty amongst employees and customers. The second example is that of Judge Gabrielle Kirk McDonald, President of the International Criminal Tribunal on war crimes in La Hague. As a woman and an African American woman, her success as a lawyer transcends her heritage and is a direct proof of the acceptance of diversity in the international arena.

Now that we have reviewed the two different aspects of leadership and the male/female type of leadership behavior, we can examine their implications on organization behavior. The male left-brain predominance, coupled with its traditional role, as a task-oriented individual may be the reason why, males are more often successful in the private sector and more specifically in line positions. They are best in a task-oriented role.

By contrast the female right-brain predominance, which is associated with her social and relationship skills prepares her for positions in the public sector and more specifically in staff positions. Women seem to be more successful in positions that are more 'relationship' oriented.

Although researchers have progressed in their identification of male and female behavioral characteristics, it does not mean that either males or females should be pigeonholed in their career path. On the contrary, these characteristics are mutually required of a great leader. There are times when the task oriented and relationship characteristics are needed at the same time. Therefore both men and women should learn the complementary skills that will make them more successful as leaders. It will also be important for organizations to recognize these characteristics and recruit their future leaders accordingly.

Why Leaders Fail?

If all leaders, men or women have the characteristics that were described above, why do so many fail? In a time when shareholders thirst for more and larger returns on their investments, increasingly CEOs find themselves under greater scrutiny. Very often bad earnings news brings about their demise and they are discarded summarily.

What is the reason for failure? This is a question, which not only intrigues CEOs, but also a much larger public. Very often it is not the lack of academic qualifications, smart or vision which causes their failure, but rather the inability to execute and deliver on commitments.

Today's successful leaders must be able to monitor both their performance and their credibility, while focusing their energy on the fundamentals of execution and delivery of commitments. The tell tale signs of incoming failure, often appear when subordinates start leaving the ship for greener pastures, and the Board of Directors starts removing its support for new strategies, often accompanied by requests for succession plans. When these signs appear it is often too late, because the support team has already started to leave the building. This is why in today's competitive environment; the execution of commitments is not the only reason for failure. While execution plays an extremely important part, it is the ability to work with people that often stands out as a major factor for failure. The inability to put people issues above strategies often is the reason for many downfalls.

Today many experts advocate the use of teams as the solution to the problems experienced by the implementation of old management models based on hierarchies. As corporations downsized, they also brought in flatter organizations, which depend upon collaboration and participation. Often the team concept is instituted without much conviction and ends up being another 'fad of the month' pronouncement by management.

For the team model to be effective we must understand that there are some underlying principles that must be observed and practiced by all the participants. The characteristics of leadership, previously discussed will be prerequisites in the implementation and success of teams. In an environment where self-managed teams are increasingly the norm rather than the exception, there will still be the need for good leaders with relationship skills.

In summary collaborative leadership can be defined as situational leadership. Where both men and women can adapt their styles based on the needs of the organization. While more men use the left side, and women use the right side of the brain, I believe that many corporate leaders have the ability to adapt to suit the appropriate circumstances. It is not a gender issue, but rather one of self-examination. Great leaders show the ability to 'shift' because it will produce better results, not because it is a means of satisfying their ego. Therefore both men and women can be equally successful as leaders in the corporate and other arenas of our society. They can both build relationships, which can produce better understanding, collaboration and teamwork.

In my opinion real teamwork is made up of these four **"Pillars":**

Trust, – the essential ingredient of collaborative management,
Empowerment, – the objective to achieving collaboration,
Acceptance of diversity of gender, culture and competencies,
Motivation done with empathy

There is such a thirst for good leadership, that under certain circumstances followers will accept do to things blindly. For that reason, leaders have a moral obligation to live up to some higher standards that their followers.

To gain maximum effort and performance from followers, good leaders must ensure that they are capable of inspiring . . .

CHAPTER 7

Trust: The Bond of relationships

"The trust most needed by organizations is trust that is earned,
then cherished."

– John O. Whitney.

WITH REORGANIZATION, RESTRUCTURING and reengineering, most workers have seen their jobs disappear or colleagues laid off. In the mean time those who are left behind are working longer hours and are required to perform at a higher standard, in many cases for less money. The 90s have seen a drastic cut back in employment in the industrialized world. Massive layoffs, in some cases, were made just to improve the bottom line while corporate leaders awarded themselves large bonuses. Workers' trust in the leadership of organizations has reached an all time low.

The key ingredient in the success of organizations is trust. Relationships are based on trust, and too often organizations have lied or broken their promises to employees, stakeholders and customers. Events of the recent past illustrate why, employees, and the public at large has lost faith in the sacred cows of old. Employees were led to believe that they had a job for life, while the public has been misled by governments about their future security and the costs of maintaining large bureaucracies. The past decade has seen an increasing number of workers laid off, while they thought that they had secured employment. By the same token we have seen the quality of certain goods fall by the way side after huge advertising campaigns had told us that the product was either safe, newer, better, or the best. We are just beginning to scratch the surface of the possibility that the tobacco industry has been hiding the effects of cigarettes on peoples' health, as evidenced by out of court settlement by Liggett & Myers Tobacco Company. That cars made by major manufacturers are constantly being recalled for defects.

Governments have continuously misinformed the public about the state of national debts and the balancing of budgets. There seems to be no end to the lies and misinformation to which we have been subjected to. Is there any trust left in governments? When was the last time you trusted governments? No wonder there is growing cynicism in the once revered institution of government, and politicians. On the corporate scene the situation is no better. It is amazing to see that organizations have not learned very much from the loss of employee trust in the last twenty years. Organizations are doing their utmost to make employees more uncomfortable in the work environment. In May 1997 the American Management Association International released a report on the increased incidence of companies' checks on employees. The findings of the report prepared in collaboration with Dr. Rosemary Orthmann stated:

"Thirty-five percent of major U.S. companies keep tabs on employees by recording their phone calls or voicemail, checking their computer files and electronic mail, or videotaping their work.

> The survey of over 900 AMA-member companies found an even larger share of firms (37%) monitoring the phone numbers that employees call and noting the duration of conversations, but not engaging in active surveillance. Additionally, 34 percent of surveyed firms videotape workspaces to counter theft, violence, or sabotage, but not specifically monitor employee performance . . .

Many employers believe that what's done on company time and on company premises is the company's business, said Eric Rolfe Greenberg, AMA's director of management studies."

The security of assets, computer data, supplies, etc., should be a prime objective for organizations. Performance of employees should be closely scrutinized. However, these new security policies that invade the privacy of employees cannot be conducive to the fostering of trust. While monitoring and supervision in an open way are advocated to maintain the integrity of the workplace, control of employees through spying should never be condoned. For this reason the whole issue of trust must be discussed and understood by all parties, employers and employees or anybody who takes part in the process.

What is trust?

The creation of a feeling of trust is essential for good leadership and followership. It is a two-way exchange, which is a corner stone of productivity, acceptance and good relationships within any type of organization and life itself. Trust and leadership are so closely related. It is not a right given to oppress or to be abused by the person in whom authority is vested. Every person affected by that trust is accountable for his actions, and therefore the principles of mutual consultation can be closely associated with the concept of working together.

Unfortunately, in large bureaucratic organizations, much of that day-to-day trust has been lost because of the large number of checks, and checkers checking checkers in the system. While not only expensive to maintain, these so-called audit systems, have had a detrimental effect on employees' morale and their trust in their respective organizations.

Trust is not something that we can expect; it is earned through truth and integrity. It is based on the clear provision of the right information, and the openness of communication. To gain peoples' trust, we require that everybody is included in the process and that no 'divide and conquer' strategy is used to reach an objective.

Bureaucratic Structures

Many employees have a low level of trust in their organizations because they no longer believe what they are told. They do not rely on management's pronouncements because; too often they have been deceived. Bureaucratic structures, which prevent good and effective communication, are by nature protective and competitive. By being competitive, we do not mean forthright competition, but an adversarial means of gathering information and controlling workers. In fact, in these organizations, promotions are often based upon rewarding some people at the expense of others. The culture stipulates that for every winner there shall be a loser. This 'win-lose' environment is Machiavellian, and people are afraid to say anything for fear that it may be reported to superiors. This is an atmosphere where backstabbing and innuendoes festers. In these organizations, people jealously guard their opinions, for fear of recriminations. The sharing of ideas is not prevalent, because recognition is not rightfully done. Plagiarism and the stealing of ideas are common in this environment. Employees take credit for their colleagues' work and the overall result is mistrust and non-collaboration.

The 'Disgruntled Employee' Syndrome

One of management's fears and a common reason for the mistrust of employees is that leaks about company problems may be made public. Often when there is a public statement about some company problems, whether it be true or false, management may initially blame it on a 'disgruntled employee'. Of course more often than not, the rumors are usually proven to be right to some extent or another. Very often when the statement made by the informant is verified, there is some truth to it. These things happen, and can have serious repercussions for the organization. Information of damaging nature, of concerns about sexual harassment, ethnic problems, quality of services or products, or even sometimes, major company policies get leaked.

Often when a 'disgruntled employee' makes information public, a major factor is ignored. Why did the employee do it? In most cases it is an employee who has been dismissed, or who feels that the company has wronged him or her in a certain way. In some cases, it may also involve a concerned employee, who no longer trusts the organization. In these days of downsizing and layoffs, this situation is becoming more frequent. It all boils down to secrecy, confidentiality, lack of information and mutual mistrust between employee and employer.

It may not be professional for the employee to divulge the company's dark secrets or misdeeds, but it is also not right for the company to mislead the public or its employees. For organizations to gain the trust of its employees and the general public, they must be forthright in their communication. Trust is gained and maintained through integrity. Organizations cannot expect loyalty from their employees or from their customers if these stakeholders are misinformed or lied to. When leaks about companies' problems are made public, organizations should stop blaming so called 'disgruntled employees' for their plight. They have only themselves to blame, first for the problem, second for covering up the problem, and third for not being trustworthy. The sad part about this is that corporations never learn. 'Whistleblowers' usually get fired or are often maligned by organizations to save face. Michael Bliss wrote:

> "People who speak out are often telling the truth, hurtful though it may be. They're not only doing their jobs properly, but there may be occasions when they have a fiduciary responsibility to state unpleasant truths in public . . . . Employers and politicians who punish us for telling the truth and surround themselves with sycophantic yes-men are heading for the ashcan of history."

While many whistleblowers may be motivated by spite, very often where their actions are truthful, these people are still treated as pariahs. In those cases where the truth is in the public interest, the whistleblower needs legal protection.

At least in the United Kingdom help is at hand. The UK government has put into place the *Public Interest Disclosure Act,* which received Royal Assent on July 02, 1998.

This Act will give employees a certain amount of job security, when they make a *'qualifying disclosure',* which in the Act is defined as *"any disclosure of information which, in the reasonable belief of the worker making the disclosure, tends to show one or more relevant failures . . ."* as described in the Act. As Martin Edwards reported:

> "The disciplinary rules may make it clear that breach of confidence will be treated as gross misconduct only where the procedure has not been followed or their complaints were made without basis or in bad faith. Such steps can help to create the right culture. But in those organisations where that culture is lacking, the new laws on public interest disclosure will prove highly significant" [3]

Other organizations and governments are creating whistleblower policies. Despite changes in the law, unfortunately whistleblowing does not necessarily mean that things are going to change. Trust is always the loser. When other employees see the treatment of one of their current or former colleagues, how can they trust management to treat them differently under similar circumstances? Blame can always be assigned, but it is the solution that really matters. Organizations, should stand up, take responsibility for their actions, and solve their problems to gain the trust of their stakeholders.

Trust as a Basis for Success

The success of an organization is based on the level of productivity. Employees' performance is central to the level of productivity of a business. Employees' performance is based on their willingness to work together to produce goods and services that are competitive, and innovative. Mutual trust is the main ingredient that can combine performance, productivity and collaborative success.

The key to engendering trust is to make workers part of the solution and treat them as responsible beings who can make a contribution to the organization. Employees should be encouraged to take risks. They should be given work that really matters, and trust them to perform to their best ability. The days of employees being driven by supervisors are virtually over. What is required in the new environment is the ability to encourage people to reach their highest level of performance through empowerment. In an ever-increasing work environment where people operate in a virtual organization relying on electronic communication, trust is going to become a more important issue for management.

In these new organizations dominated by technology and communication gadgets, face-to-face communication is rapidly disappearing. To manage in this new environment will require that organizations run themselves on trust rather than control. Virtual organizations need a new 'credo' to manage trust, because technology alone will not be enough. Let us look at some new management approaches to trust.

In organizations where a high degree of trust exists, at their best, teams and individuals, need very little supervision and management. What they need are good leaders. People control is not one of the prerequisites of the leadership function. Trust is gained through effective leadership that demonstrates commitment, the ability to assess and change behavior when required, and most of all shows, an affinity for seeking out the ideas of subordinates. Leadership that promotes a positive environment enhances trust. Leadership must allow for errors to be made and corrected so that they don't happen again. When people feel that they are always expected to make mistakes, they will make them. The way a manager handles failures will determine the future behavior of his and her subordinates. People who are punished instead of being helped will almost inevitably be reluctant to make more decisions in the future.

Leaders today must be able to build interdependence within their areas of responsibility. In order to build interdependence and trust among teams, leaders must start with themselves. They must learn to trust others, by allowing them to make decisions for themselves, and delegate more tasks to lower levels of employees. At Semco, the leader Ricardo Semper runs a company built on trust and freedom, not fear. Jaclyn Fierman (1995) reported:

> "Semco employees truly run their own company. They wear what they want, choose their own bosses, and come to and go as they please. A third of them actually set their own salaries, with one crucial hitch. They have to reapply for their jobs every six months. Production workers evaluate their higher-ups once a year and post the scores. If a manger's grade is consistently low, he or she steps down." [4]

In fact, in today's organizations, leaders do not control people anymore; they are required to help employees to higher performance through coaching and building trust. This is achieved through **Leadershift,** the ability to allow people to be themselves in order to gain the maximum collaboration for the accomplishment of mutually agreed upon objectives.

Feelings

As technology proliferates in the working environment – office, manufacturing plant etc., people are moving apart. In many instances, workers do not even come to work in an office where the organization operates. Increasingly, employees work from home and telecommute. In the global world of business, geographical flexibility makes it possible for people to work together while operating continents apart. Therefore, in these instances, workers have very little face-to-face interaction with their co-workers.

In these virtual organizations, it is important that some form of gathering is undertaken to bring these people together, some form of interaction is necessary to build trust. When people can associate a face to the task it is easier to relate to the person and his/her work. Feelings and the use of our other senses must be brought back into the work environment.

Companies that operate with a high degree of communication technology across boundaries should get their people together either to work as teams or hold an annual gathering to give employees the opportunity to meet each other. It is said that 'hi-tech' must be balanced by high-touch in order to build high-trust organizations. The meeting of employees in these circumstances is more about process than tasks. It is a means to get workers to know each other, provide them with an opportunity to put a face to the voice or the everyday e-mail. Corporate retreats and gatherings at resorts is a good way to get people together to not only reinforce corporate goals and objectives and to formulate new strategies, but to add a personal touch to the organization. Organizations which increasingly use high technology should endeavor to promote interaction and personal contact at least once a year, if not more frequently.

Bonding

Organizations are moving toward self-managed teams, which are in effect small organizations within a larger one. Trust becomes an integral part of achieving and delivering specified results. However, this type of organizational structure can also bring with it some problems. If self-managed teams become too independent, there may be occasion when relations between teams and the whole organization can become strained.

In order to avoid this possible conflict, it is necessary that some form of bonding takes place. The idea of corporate vision and mission statements is one way of dealing with this potential problem. 'Stated common goals' and objectives which binds the smaller units to the grander scheme of the whole organization is one way to create trust and harmonization

Education

The creation of teams and self-managed units generates a federal structure that works under some form of devolution of power. In order to survive in this environment, both teams and individuals must have the ability to alter, abolish and re-create themselves when circumstances change. The survival of organizations in a fast paced and rapidly changing environment is based on the ability of their people to be flexible. Employees must keep themselves abreast of change, learning new skills, exploring new opportunities and experimenting with new technologies. Trust is the answer to create a learning culture, where individuals are allowed to renew and revitalize themselves. A culture where there are no limits put on employees' abilities to educate themselves in new skills that help them become more adaptable and flexible.

Limits

Unrestricted and unlimited trust is always desirable; however in the real world it is not realistic. In collaborative management, empowerment has become the basis for the new work environment. While trust is a major part of empowerment, it does not mean that power should be limitless. Trust, under these circumstances, means the confidence in the abilities and the commitment of employees to meet goals and objectives set out by the organization. The success of empowerment depends on the clear definition of goals and objectives, to provide a set of reference points for the participants. When goals are clearly defined, teams and individuals can be left alone to perform the specified tasks. As Ron Archer said:

> "Before empowerment can really happen the conduit of trust has to be established through which authority and power will be transferred."[5]

Trust becomes control after the event, when performance is assessed. Empowerment through trust, within limits, provides the freedom to perform without restrictions to solve problems.

Toughness

Trust in organizations, not only needs leadership, but also requires a greater need for people who can work in open structures. What this means, is that the selection of people to work under these circumstances becomes very important. While recruiters are not going to be right in their selection every time, it is important that those employees who cannot perform be let go. In old large bureaucratic organizations, when people could not perform, they were booted-up, in many instances perpetuating the problem, but at another level or in a different place. Too often, incompetence in these organizations was rewarded, by promotion either upwards or laterally. The result under these circumstances was that management very quickly lost the trust of its employees. Trust must be fair, and at the same time ruthless. Management must ensure that it administers policies with fairness to gain and maintain the trust of its employees.

Employees are not machines; they are more like athletes who are striving to accomplish a goal. Like athletes, employees will strive on their own to achieve their level of competence as set by expectations, not the level to which they are driven by the old management style. Today's better-educated workforce does not require supervisors to monitor its every move and actions. Employees need supervisors who trust the skills and abilities for which they were hired in the first place. The new employees require a coach who will direct their actions towards their achievement and the organization's goals. To gain employees' trust, managers must concentrate on people-issues, feelings, intuitions, and emotions – the type of qualitative things that produces self-fulfillment. The use of qualitative, instead of quantitative measurements is more conducive to an environment of collaboration. In contrast the old methods, which use quantitative measurements, are too adversarial and engender mistrust. Although good managers will also use the quantitative things such as – control, certainty, and predictability, in the future they will do so to a lesser extent. The employees themselves will do it more effectively. As long as they are trusted to be responsible, they will also become accountable.

As we change to a more participative style, trust and integrity will become more important. Unfortunately, for far too long corporations have believed that both trust and loyalty could be obtained through financial motivation alone. Trust and loyalty, cannot be bought, they must be earned.

It is essential that trust be built gradually to the point that criticism is not a threat to the individual. This starts with the reciprocal trust between management and the workforce. In fact **Trust** is so important for the success of collaborative management that it should be treated on its own. I believe that **Trust** can be achieved and maintained through the following five principles:

Transfer of information to get action,
Rewards must be equitable, and measurements of performance should reflect strategies
Use employees' creativity to achieve innovation and gain competitiveness
Support employees needs, aspirations and desires for self-fulfillment
Team decisions, should be achieved through consensus and conflict resolution, and collaboration

How we can gain that trust in the new work environment will be explored in greater details in Chapters 11 to 15.

Most people are willing to contribute if they feel that they are trusted to perform to the best of their abilities. Now that you know the importance played by trust in relationships, it is time that we allow others to function on their own. "How do I do that?" you may ask. Simple, if you learn the secrets of true . . .

CHAPTER 8

Empowerment; the art of 'letting go'

"We place bold bets on the people we hired and then we give them the
freedom, indeed push them, to make bold bets too."
– Ed. McCracken.

"Your ability to translate authority to effective power comes from your
willingness to accept responsibility and to act responsibly."
– Paul J. Meyer.

UNDER THE OLD work environment, control was perceived to be the effective way to manage people. Large organizations often had multiple layers of supervision in order to implement control over different levels of the organization. Managers, supervisors, coordinators, etc., were the titles used to establish the hierarchical order. People management was usually done through procedures and policies, very often inflexible and bound by red tape. Of course, under these circumstances, no one was willing to ask or comment in order to effect change. Secrecy and confidentiality were the norm and information was given on 'a need to know' basis. In the new participative work environment, empowerment becomes the central element of leadership.

What is Empowerment?

Leaders do not have to control in order to influence people. They do so through deeds and behavior. The success of great leaders is to lead by example, and comes from the ability to let people lead themselves. Successful leaders don't do, they allow people to do. Empowerment is not letting workers run amuck with their own ideas, but rather influence them to take responsibility.

People have their own standards and have their own expectations of their performance. If given the opportunity to assess their performance, workers usually will set standards that are much higher than what is expected of them. In a collaborative environment, where empowerment is used, often workers find additional work to do when they are not busy; they help their colleagues to accomplish their tasks. Empowerment is the leadership style, which guides the worker towards self-leadership. It allows workers to take responsibility for their actions, performance and results.

Kouzes and Posner wrote:

> "What is often called empowerment is really just taking off the chains
> and letting people loose. Credible Leaders in this sense are liberators." [1]

Through, the use of training systems that allow for independence rather than dependence, the organization provides workers with a means to empower themselves. Through the introduction of certain behaviors, workers acquire skills that promote self-leadership.

The old leadership style used control as a central part of people management. However, control can be self-imposed. (See**Fig.1**).While many experts prefer the team approach, they often forget about the customer, in this case the employee. To this regard another way to better deal with the situation is to use the reverse pyramid model. Which is based on Employee Self-supported control – Contrast the old fashioned hierarchical company control with the inverted pyramid model Imposed control results in compliance, not commitment. Of course under imposed control tasks were achieved and goals were met – but were these goals exceeded and tasks performed to the point of excellence?

FIGURE 1.
The Inverted Pyramid Model

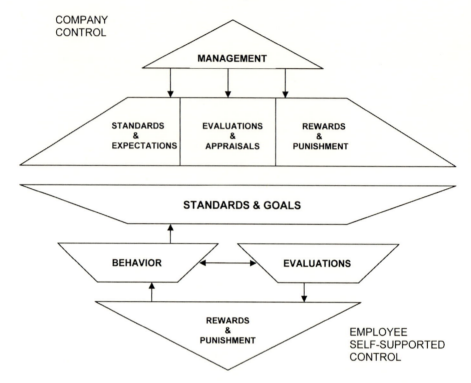

People have their own expectations of performance; they will react positively or negatively in response to their evaluations. When control is imposed, the targets are usually set. Workers will perform according to those set norms and be satisfied with the prescribed results. They are like robots that perform tasks according to expected and pre-set results and they do not feel compelled to exceed those limits. As Congor wrote:

> "Empowering, like visioning and uniting, cannot be done to people;
> they themselves must believe that they can do it."[2]

Therefore imposed control does not unleash excellence from workers. Empowerment, on the other hand is the act of recognizing that worker's self-leadership is an opportunity towards the accomplishment of excellence, and not a threat to vested authority or to organizational control. Mentoring, as we shall see in Chapter 14, plays an important role in this process.

To become more competitive, organizations should exercise management's prerogative to influence workers to lead themselves. The time has arrived for workers to become part of the decision-making process that allows them to have a say in how they perform and achieve the goals of the organization. Globalization and international competition have increased the reasons why workers should be given the opportunity to achieve excellence. Commitment, rather than compliance, is the path to higher productivity and quality, management should facilitate instead of stifling workers through control. It is said that 'giving a person a fish will feed him for the day, but showing him how to fish will feed himself for a lifetime.' The time to allow employees 'to fish' has arrived.

When to Empower?

When deciding to embark on a program of employee empowerment, attention should be paid not only to the strategies but also to the timing implementation of such a program. It will be erroneous to think that empowerment is exclusive from control. No matter how much self-management is encouraged, there are control parameters that continue to exist. Controls in the form of measurements and benchmarks, as well as the establishment of task boundaries is always found in any successful environment, and is often desired by workers as a means of feedback.

Of course time is a very important factor to take into consideration. If there is a crisis to deal with, it is very unlikely to be the best time to start empowerment. Such a program is best undertaken when time is available to communicate and articulate management's intentions and visions in detail. It is important to allow for a period of reflection and pondering by the staff to fully let them appreciate what this concept is all about. This approach is important because not all the people will jump at the idea of taking responsibility and self-management. The training aspect is crucial to the success of empowerment, and because it is generally behavioral, the process takes time. The development of employees should be encouraged, and viewed as a long-term investment.

Implementation is usually easier in an environment where tasks are somewhat unstructured. Where the tasks are of a creative, intellectual and analytical nature it is more likely that the concept will achieve success. Knowledge workers, for example take very well to the concept. This is one reason why, in the competitive computer industry the concept of empowerment and self-management is encouraged and very widely used. With the advent of 'telecommuting', where workers are away from their supervisors, empowerment is taking place at a faster rate. As business logistics and the needs of workers change, organizations must adapt and recognize the benefits of empowerment, and identify when to implement it. I advise caution in the timing and implementation of the empowerment concept. I must also point out that organizations should also recognize the ability of workers to learn and adapt to circumstances if given the right tools, skills, environment and parameters.

How to Empower?

Empowerment should be viewed as a two-way street. Both employer and employee should become partners in the process. The best way to look at this concept is to use a credit card as an example. The employer issues a '*credit card*' with no spending limit to the employee. The employee, in turn accepts the credit card, with certain conditions and parameters attached to it. This becomes an agreement between the employer and the employee as to the degree of responsibility and the latitude for making and taking decisions under particular circumstances. This process enables the employee to make decisions pertaining to his/her immediate working environment.

The idea of a '*no limit*' agreement provides the employee with an incentive to take risks and make decisions. The employer in turn agrees to give more responsibility and allow the employee to extend his/her powers of initiative to increase his/her contribution to the organization, without having to resort to a higher level of approval, on every issue. This concept provides employees with greater and immediate job satisfaction, as well as, reduces red tape within the organization.

In order to make this system work, organizations, must have clearly defined policies and ensure that mistakes are corrected immediately. The idea of a contract between employer and employee makes it more formal and provides both parties with a degree of commitment.

Why Empowerment?

In the old hierarchical structures of the past, employees were controlled through different layers of management and levels of supervision. Under those circumstances, supervisors were deemed to be more knowledgeable due to an enormous amount of experience either in the industry or through education. In today's fast changing world, technology and better-educated workers are making the old maxims of management redundant. Today many workers are better educated and have more skills than their "so called" supervisors. In fact increasingly more workers believe it is so. In a 1998 survey conducted by Inc. Magazine/Gallup, it was revealed that:

> 33% of American workers said that their boss is **more** intelligent than they are. And 11% of American workers said that their boss is **less** intelligent than they are

In this new environment, it is imperative to recognize that the old authoritarian methods of supervision no longer 'cut the mustard'. Knowledge workers are often more committed to their profession rather than the organization they work for. The younger generation of workers has different needs and is certainly no longer attached to one organization for life. Today's workers are looking for the next opportunity to put their skills to better use, either within the existing organization or from the competition. The old method of promotion up the ladder, no longer exist because of restructuring and flatter organizations. One way of retaining highly skilled and valuable employees is through empowerment. By making them part of the solution, instead of only being a part of the problem, the organization has a lot to gain in the form of higher productivity and employee job satisfaction.

Workers today do not want to be told what to do; they prefer an atmosphere where their ideas are listened to, and where open discussions are encouraged. They do not always seek approval for their ideas, but they need management to tell them that their ideas are considered useful. Empowerment is essential in an environment dominated by knowledge workers. In the old days, tasks were assigned to specific positions, and the supervisor would just tell the employee to perform the task. Although there was some guidance more frequently the tasks had to be done according to certain strict procedures and policies. Today, the better-educated workers want to be more proactive, they want to inject some of their own personality and skills in the performance of their job. In other words, today workers ask: "If you want me to do it, let me in on it." These workers thrive on creativity and need to participate in the decision making process, especially when they are asked to be part of the implementation.

Employee Self-Leadership

One of the characteristics of great leadership is the ability to influence others. However, the success of any leader depends on the willingness of people to follow. It is therefore incumbent upon the leader to guide followers in such a way as to enable them to direct and learn for themselves. Under a scenario where followers are allowed to function for themselves instead of being commanded to perform, it is easier to achieve followership. In this case the role of the leader changes into one of coach, guide, facilitator, replacing the old role often associated with control and authority. This environment results in significant benefits for the organization in terms of increased performance, higher productivity, innovation, and of course self-fulfillment for all participants – leaders as well as followers.

Of course not everyone is a self-leader. People are not always born with the characteristics required to be a self-leader, however under the right circumstances and guidance these traits can be learnt. A born leader can be taken to mean that such an individual knows it all. However, I think that no matter how well-developed an individual's leadership qualities are, an integral part of the skills of a leader is to take direction from his/her boss and also take the input of other people within his/her peer group and subordinates. The leader and the organization must provide the followers with the opportunity to learn and practice those traits that are required for self-leadership. The success of employee self-leadership depends on the behavior of management.

In most cases, people are cognizant of their behavior and often are able to manage their actions and behavior. First the leader must feel empowered, to be able to empower others. A leader without self-confidence cannot inspire others to greatness. Organizations must promote self-leadership in order to allow the feeling of empowerment to reach every single employee. People who feel empowered contribute more and produce extraordinary results. The achievement of excellence does not come by easily it requires practice and encouragement. The environment must provide support and promote personal excellence. During the learning process, employees should be encouraged to use a set of strategies to help achieve personal excellence, and these strategies may include:

Mission Statement and Goal Setting

Personal excellence starts with knowing what you want, and a personal mission statement should help in learning about oneself and knowing what must be done. The setting of goals is personal and helps to focus on a finishing line. Employees should be encouraged to set short-term tasks, and long-term, career goals. There is no glory in achieving meaningless goals. The goals should be challenging, specific and yet achievable in order to provide the maximum effect. *Examples:*

> Short-term – Task: Spending less time on the phone.
> Long-term – Career: Take night courses to get a degree.

Armed with a mission statement and a set of goals, the empowered employee can enter the realms of self-management and self-fulfillment.

Managed Environment

Surroundings, sight, sounds and people, etc influence behavior. Employees can manage their behavior by becoming aware of their environment and make use of everyday cues to help them improve. They can identify the things that stimulate and irritate them and eliminate the bad and keep the desirable.

The office can be decorated with things that stimulate performance. Use light, upbeat music in the background to stimulate the senses, and positive quotations and posters to create positive reinforcements. Where employees have offices, allow them to personalize their environment, within reason. They can decorate their allocated area, with personal objects, which will make them feel more at home and thus create a personal atmosphere. Allow employees to manage time through cueing strategies, which will make them more effective and productive. Employees should surround themselves with positive people, to keep themselves in a positive frame of mind.

The Use of Feedback

To pursue continuous improvement, there must be a means of checking the desired performance. When a task has been completed, written and/or verbal feedback is essential in order to provide a road map about the task, the skills used and the final result. This strategy can provide the necessary observance for change in undesirable behaviors that are preventing progress and pinpoint the desirable behaviors and their positive use and effect. Keeping a diary or other form of record is a good means of keeping track of progress. A road map of personal success and failure should be kept. If and when the undesirable behavior returns, a quick check of the records can show the road back to the desired behavior.

Practice

Success cannot be achieved without rehearsal or practice. Successful artists and athletes practice for hours, days, months and years to become proficient at what they do. Behavior is no different, as only practice will provide long lasting improvements.

To achieve excellence requires the same dedication, which athletes and others demonstrate. In the work environment, a good presentation requires good material and rehearsal. After all it is a performance, similar to an actor on stage. Role-playing is a great way to practice. In learning organizations, teams undertake field trips to public parks and other inspiring places and take part in out-of-bounds exercises to simulate events that require teamwork, collaboration, and participation.

Self-Rewards and Self-Punishment

People usually are well aware of their successes and failures. They know when their behavior is desirable and undesirable. A feedback method provides an excellent way of tracking behavior. It is also important to reinforce good behavior with rewards and also punish poor behavior. In the empowered environment, the self-managed employee can administer both rewards and punishment.

Rewards can be used as motivational tools to encourage desired behaviors. They can take the form of personal pats on the back, to spending a day off from work after finishing a difficult undertaking. Rewards can help promote and sustain motivation, effort and continuous self-improvement.

Punishments on the other hand are an integral part of the process. They usually are in the form of mental and cognitive nature. However, the application of punishment must not become habitual as it may cause depression and undermine motivation and self-improvement. Once again the feedback method provides a guide on the frequency and results of the behavior. The record keeping should be used to indicate if behavior and/or punishment are too frequent, and whether perhaps professional help should be sought.

Worker Independence

The new leader has a responsibility to provide his/her followers with the ability to move from dependence on management to independence. The essence of empowerment is to help employees become more responsible for their actions and become accountable for them. The leader's role is to use guidance and encouragement to facilitate the process of self-management. One of the fundamental objectives of worker independence is to achieve better productivity, while employees gain job satisfaction.

However, not all people are adept at being independent. In fact this is supported by Tom Melohn who writes:

> "All too often, worker empowerment fails because the employees won't take the responsibility for the results of their work. Unfortunately, not everyone will assume that burden."[3]

If this statement is true, the leader's role is to identify the better employees and let them proceed without supervision, while guiding and coaching employees who are less able to manage themselves. This also implies that a leader should possess different styles and apply each one to the maturity level of the employee being supervised.

Coaching is a word commonly used to describe one of the desired competencies of leaders in this changing work environment, however very few managers really know how to coach. Coaching is about knowing when to control and when to give up control. Success is usually dependent upon excellence, and excellence is attained through personal growth. Good coaches allow risk taking, because one cannot grow without making mistakes. As long as mistakes are corrected and used as an opportunity for improvement, workers will strive for independence and responsibility.

In sports, successful coaches are the ones who are adept at bringing the best out of their athletes on a consistent basis. Coaches know how to recruit the best and they allow a certain amount of freedom with a predetermined plan of action. Coaches who are too inflexible do not get the best out of their athletes. They may gain production from them but not necessarily excellence. For example, some years ago, in my capacity as a part-time tennis coach, I had the opportunity to work with a very talented junior player, Bobby Havlacek. This talented player played with two-handed grips on both his forehand and backhand strokes. His right hand was placed at the top of the grip while his left hand was placed at the bottom of the grip, just as a left-hander would hold his racquet for a two-handed backhand. Bobby went to train with a very reputed and talented coach. After two weeks he quit the program and came to see me. He told me that his coach wanted him to change his grip and that he could no longer play for him. In our conversation I asked him what seemed to be the problem. He told me that this coach wanted him to change his grip by placing his right hand at the bottom of the grip, just as a right-handed player would do for his double-handed backhand. At this stage I did not see any problems with the coach's request. I decided to hit a few balls with him and saw no apparent problems with his stroke production. So I asked him, why he would not change his grip to the more conventional one, and he replied that he felt uncomfortable. So we continued to practice with his 'normal' grip. Later it occurred to me to ask him whether he was right or left handed. Although he served right handed, he told me that he was left-handed but learned to play tennis two-handed. Of course it was more comfortable for him to use a left-hander's grip since he was left-handed by nature. I continued to help him with his game without changing his preferred grip. He went on to be a provincial junior champion and a representative of the 'Vandals' of Idaho University.

Execution by the best athletes should be left to their own abilities and personal skills. Coaches must identify the strengths and weaknesses of athletes or workers. Coaches should hone their peoples' strength and make them better, while working on the weaknesses for improvement. The talents of athletes are allowed to come out on every occasion. The objective is always to obtain the maximum benefit for the success of the team. Coaches encourage and demand support from all members of the team, and they always take responsibility for the failures of their team. In this atmosphere of trust, risk taking is allowed and success is rewarded.

Designing Tasks

Empowerment gives a sense of satisfaction and meaning to one's job. Employees should be given the opportunity to have pleasurable and meaningful experiences while performing their tasks. One of the ways to achieve job satisfaction and administer self-rewarding experiences is to be given the ability to redesign one's job to reach self-fulfillment. To make work more pleasurable, employees should identify what aspects of the job they enjoy, and increase these aspects as much as possible. This allows employees to take more responsibility in incremental phases.

There are many different ways of performing tasks, and individuals usually are as different in their approaches as their behavior. For example there are people who perform better at night than early in the morning. People tend to do work in different ways and perhaps in different sequences. We must recognize this difference and allow individuals, within certain parameters, the latitude to redesign their tasks. This approach allows employees to adapt to the elements of their work environment that provide self-control and a sense of competence and pleasure.

However, there are limitations to how much individuals can redesign their work to make it more pleasurable. The constraints of the job must be taken into account, and a better way would be to redesign by adjusting very small incremental steps in the processes. Attempting change in one large step may create chaos, confusion and eventually lead to disappointment. If workers are given the opportunity to make their jobs more enjoyable, they will also take more responsibility for their actions while seeking job satisfaction. The significant difference under this approach is that it is no longer incumbent upon management to be responsible for minor changes in the work environment of individuals.

Culture

The components of culture can become a powerful tool for management's search and implementation of high-performance and excellence in the work environment. The challenge is to create an atmosphere that promotes excitement, motivation and becomes a way of life unique to the organization.

Although the objective of empowerment may be the loosening of control by management, it is imperative that the upper echelons of the organization play an important role in its implementation. The values, norms and beliefs encapsulated within the corporation's culture provide meaning, purpose and commitment for all participants. Culture becomes the guiding force for expected behavior to achieve the successful implementation of strategies. Therefore, executives have a responsibility to pass on the appropriate culture they would like to see exhibited across the organization. For example: in a customer-focused organization, employees are empowered to satisfy customers' needs. *Four Seasons Hotels and Resorts*, the 'gold standard' of the hospitality industry practices this philosophy. As Ms. Cherry Kam, Director of Public Relations, Four Seasons Hotel, Toronto once explained:

> "We are empowered to make decisions right there and then, right down to the line staff. We first make sure the customer is satisfied at the very moment. Then the Manager will support the position taken"[4]

In an empowered environment, the culture will be one of participation, where human resource management becomes an integral part of the overall strategic planning process of the organization. The new strategy will be to provide workers with an environment that enables them to motivate themselves without much bureaucratic control.

Many believe that with de-layering of organizations and flatter hierarchies the need for 'managers' will disappear. This is simply not true. There will always be a need for the management of tasks, and more importantly the management of relationships. Even in an empowered environment some management will still be required. The role of managers may change from controllers to facilitators. However some form of management will still be required. The skills and competencies required will vary from organization to organization. Organization culture will determine which type of manager will be required to achieve a blend of 'tasks' and 'relationships' management in the empowered environment.

Barriers to Implementation

Attempts to introduce empowerment fail because of a lack of communication and clear guidance and support. The strategies are often introduced 'too much, too soon' and creates confusion and may lead to chaos, resulting in failure. Resistance to change is often the result of miscommunication, and in some circumstances may lead to some employees 'testing the waters' to see whether management really means what they say. The implementation of an empowerment program must make space for errors and failures. Participants must be provided with the opportunity to learn from their failures. The executive's eagerness to see immediate results may also be a factor, which can contribute to failure. Patience, is not only a virtue, but is an integral part of the implementation process of empowerment.

In this Chapter we have reviewed the different factors that make or break empowerment. The concept of empowerment is a key element of collaborative management. Although it is mostly put forward as an alternative for the old control strategies of management often found in hierarchical organizations, the concept can be introduced in all types of organizations; from government committees and commissions, to volunteer organizations.

Empowerment is not magic; it is the art of 'letting go'. It means that those in power must relinquish control to enable the achievement of excellence by subordinates. Empowerment is a concept that allows for participation in an open environment and encourages the exchange of ideas. This idea is better expressed by Wille and Hodgson who wrote:

> "To feel empowered means that we feel our survival is in our own hands; we don't blame others or speak all the time of those vague entities called 'they'." [4]

Empowerment produces higher performance, which results in the achievement of excellence. In a continuously shrinking world, we are bound to meet and work with people who are different from us. They may differ in culture, education and very often have different ideas from ours. True empowerment allows the free flow of ideas, supplemented by growing harmony in organizations. To ensure that it happens, we cannot ignore the importance of . . .

CHAPTER 9

Acceptance of Diversity

"If we were the same, we wouldn't be different."
– Adam Hanft.

"We are more alike, than we are different."
– David Brinkley.

"The future of the human race lies in maintaining its diversity
and turning that diversity to its advantage."
– Edward T. Hall.

IN TODAY'S WORK environment, acceptance takes a very prominent position in the corporate culture. As we move towards a more global environment, not only is it necessary to understand that we have workers from different genders, but also from different ethnic backgrounds, different national cultures, different values, beliefs and moral standards. In the new environment of participative management, corporations must take diversity in the workforce into consideration, more so for corporations operating in the international arena. It is imperative for management to account for all differences that exist in the work environment in order to recruit and promote its workers. Sally J. Walton (1994) better expresses this point of view:

"When we speak of cultural diversity in the workplace, we're not just speaking of nationalities or ethnic groups, but also of age, gender, race, religion, sexual orientation, physical abilities, where you live(metropolitan/small town/rural locations), plus subcultures within any of these categories based on occupation, education, and personality."[1]

We must also accept that people have different levels of education and different competencies. Organization should identify peoples' best skills and use them for the benefit of the individual worker and the organization. We shall look at several factors that create the importance for 'acceptance' in the work environment.

Mistakes and Failures

One of the main features and drawbacks of large hierarchical and autocratic organizations has been the total aversion to mistakes and failures. In these organizations, any mistakes big or small is summarily punished and viewed as a major failure. In this prevailing work environment it has been extremely difficult to gain workers' participation and enhance creativity. The fear of failure is instilled in workers and prevents them from being innovative. Often mistakes and failures are punished through wage reductions or in the longer term, the inability to be promoted.

An admired trait of leadership is risk-taking. Many, if not all, successful leaders have demonstrated the ability to take risk and in so doing have supported their subordinates to do the same. Acceptance of mistakes and failure by these leaders has often been the catalyst for worker innovation and creativity, and has also resulted in learning experiences. Organizations that accept failures and mistakes, within certain benchmarks, often are the most successful. In this type of corporate culture, people who make mistakes are not viewed as pariahs, but are given a chance to improve themselves. The acceptance of mistakes as part of the learning process for future improvement removes the fear of failure, and allows workers to participate more openly in the running of the business, In this atmosphere, creativity and innovation usually thrive.

Competencies

Nowadays there is a lot of talk about competencies. What are they anyway? In general, competencies can be defined as the set of critical skills employees require for a given job specification or classification in an organization in order to perform effectively. We must accept that people have skills, which are sometimes unique, sometimes similar and in most cases different to some degree. As we move into a more competitive world, not only personal competencies but corporate 'core competencies' become more critical. It is also argued that distinct human resource practices can drive the uniqueness of corporate competencies that differentiates products and services from the competition. If this is so, it is therefore incumbent upon management to provide a means of selection, recruitment and training that will provide the organization with the required competency base to enable competitiveness and success.

During the downsizing trend of the past many workers have been let go because they did not have the right competencies for a changing environment. However corporations forgot that most of them did not train or prepare these workers to acquire these needed competencies. In an ever-changing world, businesses must recognize that to remain competitive their employees must be continuously trained to maintain and acquire new competencies. Individual competencies must be identified to match the core competencies of the corporation. It is no longer good enough to hire people with certain competencies and then discard them when those same competencies, which made them contributors to the bottom line, become obsolete. Adequate training and time to adapt must be allowed for. Corporations must accept the responsibility for the provision of opportunities for their employees to learn, acquire, and improve the right competencies.

Diversity

My own background and origin makes me a quasi authority on the subject of diversity. I was born in Mauritius, a tiny little island in the Indian Ocean, of mixed parents of French, Chinese and African origin. I was brought up in a diverse society made up of East Indians, Africans, French, Chinese and mixed blood people. Very early in my life, I learned about diversity of language, culture and ethnicity. My education was in French complemented by English and my professional and postgraduate studies were undertaken in England. While, I cannot say that I have overtly been subjected to racial discrimination, I can say that I have been subjected to systemic discrimination. As a Canadian, my English qualifications were often used as a reason for not breaking certain glass ceilings in my work environment. While Canada, prides itself of being a tolerant society, very often systemic discrimination, which is prevalent in many organizations, is dismissed as trivial, and non-existent. This is far from the truth, as many lawsuits come to the fore in both the private and public sectors. The acceptance of diversity in the work place will play a more important role as we become more global in our strategies.

As more women and ethnic minorities enter the work force, it is time for corporations to face the fact that the old maxim of promotion based on the gender and color should be replaced. I am not advocating a blank acceptance of 'affirmative action' but rather a more equitable approach to recruiting and promotion in the new work environment. In addition, employment equity as we know it, often discriminates against white males. To rectify a wrong, we should not be using another wrong. Talent is gender neutral and color blind. My precept is based on the fact there are several factors apart from just demographics that make this change necessary.

The first one that comes to mind is that by accepting more women and minorities in the work place, corporations have a larger pool of talent to choose from. It is not only moral to stop the discrimination along gender and racial lines, but extremely important to reflect the actual demographics of the population. Meritocracy should be based solely on competencies and abilities. By recognizing the diverse workforce and hiring according to merit, the organization can better represent and serve its customers. Many corporations have moved towards acceptance of diversity and have started special programs to promote women within their organizations. Let us look at one example reported by Himelstein and Anderson Forest(1997):

> "Simply establishing objectives, however, wasn't enough. So, Motorola, revamped its succession planning-focusing first, unlike other companies, on its most senior staff. Top managers now must supply names of the three people most likely to replace them. The first is the manager who would fill the job in an emergency. The second slot is for someone who could be groomed for the job in three to five years. The new third spot is dedicated to the woman or minority closest to being qualified for the position. Managers are expected to give that third person opportunities to get the experience needed to merit the promotion. As a result, women have moved into the first or second slots approximately 75 of the company's 300 most prized jobs." [1]

It is important for corporations to look at their hiring and succession planning practices to include more women and minorities in the upper echelons of their organizations. They will then be able to attract the best from all walks of life. When people see evidence that the top of the organization looks like them, they will be more willing to join.

Globalization

As more companies move their business activities to other countries, there will be a need to recruit and hire more local staff. In the past expatriates, staffs who were moved from the head office to be stationed abroad occupied many positions in multinationals operating in foreign countries. In the beginning this strategy made sense, but as education becomes more international, increasingly nationals are qualified to take up senior management positions in companies operating outside industrialized countries. The advantages of hiring locally are numerous. The local staff bring with them instant knowledge of the culture, market, customer preferences and understanding of the political environment. There is no transition or adaptation period required for these local managers, and their appointment shows the local government that their citizens are making a contribution to their economy. There is less friction, caused by nationalistic views, and increased goodwill for the corporation. In this case, acceptance means that the corporation has recognized the different culture, norms, values and customs of its local staff.

Corporations must remember that 'minorities' under these circumstances are in reality the majority. Human resource policies and strategies, in foreign operating centers, must reflect the local culture and traditions. In industrialized countries where many immigrant entrepreneurs are increasingly playing a greater role in the growth of the economy, it is important to recognize their contribution. Immigrant employees and entrepreneurs can add a new dimension to the competitiveness of corporations. As Nabiha Atallah said:

> "I would especially like to see more businesses view immigrant entrepreneurs as a potential resource for international trade. It is an obvious fit, because they know the language, they know the market, and they know the people." [2]

Gender Difference – Women

Gradually, men are more willing to share housework with their partners, either by helping in the kitchen and other chores or spending more time with the children. As this trend continues, it is time for corporations to do the same thing and allow women to take more responsibility in the work environment. Women in the workforce are no less qualified than men, but are handicapped by some common beliefs that must be taken out of the workplace. For example, there are some general assumptions, that women for instance do not like traveling, or do not like informal gatherings. These are some excuses, which have sometimes excluded women from promotion to higher executive levels. Instead we must recognize that there exists some significant differences among the genders and learn to accept them. We shall look at some of these differences in characteristics later.

Gender Difference – Men

As mentioned earlier, men are increasingly taking more responsibilities at home. They share more household work with their partners because they recognize that with a working wife, they can no longer expect to be looked after hand and foot. The two-income family seems to be here to stay; it also means that with more women entering the workforce, more sharing will have to be done.

However, if this trend of job sharing and diversification of duties is done at home, it is inconceivable that it cannot be done in the work place. Men have to start accepting that women have a role to play in the growth and success of businesses. What they have to recognize is that there are areas where women can make significant contributions and that they deserve to be recognized for their efforts. By not accepting the impact of women's contribution in the work environment, corporations largely ran by men, have lost many qualified women to small businesses.

In fact, women have started the majority of small entrepreneurial businesses in the past 15 years. The growth of the home-based business is mainly due to women, often forced by necessity, to use their creativity to find a niche for their abilities and ideas. Small businesses are creating jobs faster than large corporations. If women manage the majority of these small businesses, how is it that major corporations could not use the talents of these women for the growth of their businesses?

One of the obstacles in breaking down gender barriers in the workplace is perhaps the lack of understanding of gender differences. We must identify these differences, identify the competencies attached to them and accept them for what they are. Executives, mostly of the male gender, must accept that male and female competencies are often the result of genetics. Male acceptance of this fact can create corporate policies, which can help bridge, the gap between the genders and maximize the use of all their employees irrespective of gender.

Gender Gap or Gender Trap?

While men and women have physical differences that are generally accepted, we also have some gender differences, which are not fully understood and therefore less acceptable. As we move into a new era of management styles, we must look at the competencies that are inherent and inherited by both genders. Perhaps a better understanding of our genetic characteristics can help change the composition of executive suites and boardrooms.

First let us look at the differences in the use of the brain. Research has shown that males are predominantly left-brain oriented, while females are generally more right-brain oriented. What this means is that males and females view things in different ways, and it may be one of the reasons why fundamental differences exist between the two genders.

Right-brain predominance is usually associated with creativity, relationships and emotion. The left-brain is predominantly associated with logic, analytical skills and solving problems. Therefore since, in general, male and females have different brain predominance we can see that males and females will generally have competencies different from each other. From this general assumption we can see why men could be better in certain jobs while women could excel at others. This difference in our preference for either the left or right side of the brain, also explains the way we think differently. Since the left-brain is associated with logic, males tend to be better at solving problems, while women who are right-brain predominant tend to be more creative. As well, men are usually more task oriented while women are often more relationship oriented. Having said that, we must not ignore that there also exist many sensitive men and many logical women.

This brings us to the point about the collaborative management trend that is gradually taking the place of authoritarian management styles usually associated with hierarchical organizations. In some places, it is suggested that teams are going to be the backbone of future organizations. Teams are based on relationships, trust and mostly on the ability of members to get along together. If this is so, there is a tremendous future for female leaders in this new era. Why? It is because women are genetically better prepared at resolving relationship issues and are best at getting people to work together without asserting undue authority. History supports this theory. Many women have been successful and made significant contributions to society in the political arena. Margaret Thatcher, Golda Meir and Indira Gandhi are but a few who come to mind. Except for a small selective number, few women have made their mark in the corporate world. One of the exceptions that come to mind is, *Ford Canada's* CEO Bobbie Gaunt. Of course there are a few exceptions where women executives have done well. The civil service and the service industries such as publishing and hospitality industries have produced excellent and very successful female leaders such as Former United States Secretaries of State Elizabeth Dole, Condoleezza Rice and Hillary Clinton, Publishing pioneers like *Cosmopolitan's* Helen Gurley Brown, Marjorie Scardino of Pearson plc., and *The Washington Post's* Katharine Graham.

The differences between the genders have made it more possible for women to excel in the civil service where the business is more involved in the relationship field – that of distributing wealth. In the corporate world it has been different because this sector is more involved in the creation of wealth, that is, more a task oriented function. By virtue of these differences, it is more likely for women to excel in staff and support positions such as Human Resources Management, Public Relations, etc. Males on the other hand are more commonly found in line positions, especially in engineering and technical corporations.

The differences mentioned above are also complementary; this is why humans have survived. However, recent statistics still show that among *Fortune* magazine's top 500 U.S. companies only 11% of corporate officers are women, and women account for just 2.5% of the top earners among the group. The most significant problem remains, that for women to be viewed as successful in the corporate world, society requires them to exhibit qualities and behavior that are more closely attributable to men. It was once said of Margaret Thatcher that: 'she was the only man in the Conservative Party'. In reality good leadership requires a blend of both male and female attributes. Great leaders must be able to make decisions based on objective reasoning, while using a more emphatic and personal way.

For both genders the requirement is for the development of a deeper appreciation of the full range of skills that influence effective leadership. While men more frequently display a more task oriented and 'progressive' approach, women on the other hand, prefer a more relationship oriented and 'conservative' approach. To achieve any progress in this area requires that not only women should acquire 'task oriented' skills, but also men should acquire the 'relationship' skills that would help them become more rounded. It is imperative that both men and women recognize, accept and develop the full range of skills required for effective leadership. Diversity means the acceptance of men and women who are able to blend the attributes of both genders. Many women have been confident and successful at using the male attributes, while many men have also recognized and used female attributes to become successful. In the past it may have been difficult for members of both genders to display each other's attributes successfully, mainly for fear of being branded by society. However, today it is becoming easier to adopt each other's traits to reach the chosen objectives of collaboration. It is only a transition, but it can be achieved by both genders.

Achieving a Diversified Workforce

Acceptance of differences within an organization is desirable, however to attain a right balance of equality is another proposition. The rank and file is not opposed to inclusion; very often it is the leadership, which is lacking to make diversity a reality. In a February 1999 survey undertaken by The National Post/ COMPAS Inc., it was interesting to note the 'yes' answers to the following two questions:

Item	Men	Women
Do women have too much power in the workplace	7%	5%
Not enough power in the workplace	57%	73%

However over the years the is a clear shift towards more women in corporate authority. Some would say that the progress is not enough; nevertheless we cannot deny that there has been progress. As Pamela Jeffery wrote in the Financial Post (December, 04, 2012): "*We are celebrating a decade of leadership at a time when the world seems to be catching up to the message we have been driving home since day one: Women are natural leaders*". This is exemplified by the latest list of Canada's top 100 women, which include Aimee Chan of Norsat International, Trudy Curran of Canadian Oil Sands Ltd., Cynthia Devine of Tim Hortons Inc., and Leslie O'Donoghue of Agrium Inc. among many others.

If organizations are serious about their employees they should be looking at ways to integrate females and minorities into their corporate structure. They should also be looking to identify the right competencies and use them into their system of meritocracy. How can organizations achieve integration?

In many companies, management uses the mentoring system to prepare employees for the next level of responsibility. It is not only enough to find internal mentors, but it is also extremely favorable to match employees with exceptional potential with external mentors. The one problem that may arise with internal mentoring is that there is 'cloning'. To please their internal mentors and achieve success, protégés may start taking all the characteristics of their protectors. This close association and transference may prevent the individual's development; remove some of the protégé's personal traits and competencies that make him or her unique. To prevent this possibility, external mentorship is advocated.

In this case, the possible internal conflicts are removed, and more importantly external mentors can be more candid with their advice. Corporations can send their brightest female prospects to such organizations as "Women's Organization for Mentoring, Education and Networking Unlimited Inc. This organization is used to help women in their quest to be successful in a male oriented business world. Through these programs, women can acquire skills like 'how to communicate in an all – male situation', and they learn to understand the subtleties of leadership which men appreciate. Often in these external mentorship programs, women can find out that they do not have to be aggressive to be successful. In effect, aggressiveness may be a root cause to upsetting both female and male co-workers. These types of mentorship programs help participants with skills and competencies that are not focused on generic leadership and management competencies, but instead provide them with an understanding of the environment.

Programs and plans to help minorities and women advance in organizations are well meaning, but to be successful they require the commitment of management. In many corporations where diversity issues are addressed as a priority, the initiative has more often than not, come from a senior executive. The commitment must be such that the diversity issue becomes part of the corporate culture so that even the champion's departure does not affect the program. To illustrate:

> "At Corning Inc., for example, some ex-employees and outside diversity experts say the issue has lost prominence since former Chairman and CEO James R. Houghton began giving up control several years ago. Although women comprise more of Corning's top earners. Diversity

seminars are offered less often and management has been distracted by financial problems, they say. Corning strongly disagrees." [4]

In other companies such as PricewaterhouseCoopers, they have instituted specific training and mentoring programs to narrow the gender gap. As an incentive they have also linked partners' bonuses to diversity issues. Texaco, is addressing the diversity issue by allowing more minorities to own dealerships and create an environment where minorities are given more opportunities within the organization. This however, only happened after the discovery of tape recordings of meetings in which executives were heard disparaging black employees, and discussing the destruction of files that could have helped the plaintiffs in their legal suit against Texaco.

Acceptance must be practiced not as a reactive but as proactive strategy. The diversity of the workforce and the globalization of business in general make it imperative for organizations to have the 'pillar' of acceptance as a core value. The practice of acceptance must be sponsored by management and rewarded when practiced. The whole idea must be included in the organization's overall strategy and can be beneficial to . . .

CHAPTER 10

Motivate with Empathy

"The difference between employees who perform well and those who
perform poorly, is not how they are paid but how they are treated."
– J. Sterling Livingston.

WHILE IT IS generally accepted
that financial rewards are perhaps
at the very top of the motivation list for employees, it is becoming apparent
that they are not the only ones. The heavy demands of the new economy put
enormous pressures on the family life of working couples. Increasingly, young
families are finding it difficult to balance a promising career with the demands of
childcare, or looking after an elderly parent. There is a need for organizations to
reevaluate their corporate culture with regards to family values.

The proliferation of knowledge workers has increased the preference for
rewards other than those, which are purely financial. In many instances, these
workers require support for their ideas and rank job satisfaction high on their
list of needs. While financial rewards are of importance, today's employees seek
other benefits from their employers. High on that list is the promise of training
and development. The other aspect that is becoming quite an issue is corporate
culture. People do not just take a job any more, because it pays well. The
environment, the culture of the organization and whether they will be treated
decently increasingly motivate them.

Employees want to be treated as individuals who have something unique to contribute to the organization. If their contribution is not unique, then they want to feel that they can contribute in a manner that is accepted and recognized for its merits. Recognition and appreciation for their efforts are the new engines for motivation. In flatter organizations, promotion up the ladder is no longer an automatic reward for performance; therefore employees seek different rewards for their accomplishments. Let us look at the factors that influence motivation and employee performance in this new environment, and identify some solutions for a better atmosphere and collaboration between management and employees.

Understanding Motivation

Over the past decade organizations, either forced or by design, have undergone many changes to remain competitive and profitable. Downsizing, layoffs, and dismissals have affected layers of employees in many organizations. Recently it was not only blue-collar workers who were affected; white-collar workers in middle management have been the largest casualties. When layoffs have been avoided, the climate has undergone radical changes and in many cases flatter organizations have meant that promotions were no longer available. These changes, of course, have led to severe demoralization among all ranks of organizations. Meanwhile, enlightened management executives search for new ways to motivate their workforce in order to become more competitive and increase productivity. Motivation of the workforce has taken a new meaning in the new corporate environment. However, as management seeks new ideas, it often still believes in the old methods, and this can be a detriment to progress. This is why, it is important for us to look at the underlying factors of motivation and understand its mechanics in order to adjust and adapt to the new environment. Richard S. Sloma provides a good definition of the elements of motivation and he defines them as:

> "**Motivation**: A need or desire that causes a person to take some action.
> **Motive:** An emotion or desire operating on a person's will and, thereby, causing it, in turn to generate action.
> **Incentive:** This applies to an external inducement (as an expected reward) inciting one to action." [1]

The above definitions are important in understanding the concept of motivation, or what really makes people 'tick'. In addition, it is also essential to understand the underlying perceptions of peoples' behaviors. As far back as the sixties, Douglas McGregor, wrote about his now famous Theory X and Theory Y, which described people's behavior in organizations. The unfortunate part is that management and workers have different beliefs and behavior, thus causing much turmoil in the work environment. Let us explain.

Theory Y believes that most people care about their jobs, wish to reach high performance through achievement. If given a chance, they will take responsibility and generally will do excellent work. Unfortunately, Theory X, which in many cases forms the basis of many organizations, believes that generally workers are lazy, irresponsible, and dependent, and that they need constant supervision. Their task and work must be divided in small pieces, controlled and constantly supervised in case they make mistakes.

Bureaucratic and hierarchical organizations have often used Theory X as the foundation for their management style. Motivation in these organizations, have been through fear, control and promotion to the next level of supervision. However, the problem lies in the fact that the culture of these organizations created workers who were rarely allowed to think for themselves and were tightly controlled in the performance of their duties. These same workers were also promoted to the next level of supervision, thus perpetuating the vicious cycle of control and lack of initiative and innovation. Many managers in this environment are not in their position of supervision because of their abilities, but rather because of tenure and organization culture that believed promotion and financial reward was the key to motivation.

In the new economy, many changes were undertaken. Restructuring introduced new technology, new processes and new knowledge workers in the working place. These changes require that management review its motivating policies to accommodate this new work environment. As mentioned before, financial motivation is no longer the determining factor, as other factors take priority in peoples' lives.

Just as the old contract, of a job for a lifetime, has gone out of the window, corporations must not expect that employee loyalty will continue to be a priority for workers. In order to motivate workers in this new environment, management must come to grips with the additional needs of today's employees. Management must understand what makes the employee of the new century tick. Motivation through fear and control, no longer works. Motivation with empathy and understanding is now the preferred order of the day. Enlightened organizations have already adopted policies that reflect this new environment. Ms Catherine Caven – Director of Human Resources, **Four Seasons Hotel** Toronto says:

> "Pride is an incredible motivator in this organization. People are so proud to work for Four Seasons. Our retention is incredibly high and our turnover is incredibly low. If you talk to anybody, at any level, you will find that pride is number one. Pride in the product, pride in the company, pride in the way we do business."

In fact what it boils down to is making employees feel good about themselves, their job and their company. In return the organization gets a happy employee committed to the organization's goals and to satisfying the customer. They are treated and respected as individuals.

I am an individual

The new knowledge workers are no longer content to be treated as members of a large organization which treats its employees as faceless people with an employee number for administrative and identification purposes. Their abilities, competencies and skills make them unique individuals within a group, and they want to be recognized as such.

They do not want Theory X applied to them and they do want their efforts recognized. They can make a contribution and they want to contribute. They have ideas, although some good and some not so good, they appreciate having these ideas heard. They want to be part of the decision-making process, especially when the outcome affects them. They are honest and take pride in what they do; they want a fair reward for an honest day's work. In other words employees want to be distinguished as individuals, anything less makes them feel inadequate, and destroys both their motivation and self-esteem.

The objective of motivation should follow a pattern of managing individuals to get the best out of them. In this context it is important that managers/supervisors work with employees to identify mutually acceptable ways to allow the employee to produce outstanding results, satisfy the organizations' goals and remain true to his or her individualism. In order to perform at peak performance, as individuals and/or team members, employees want to know what is expected of them.

Expectations

For motivation to have a positive impact, both the employee and the employer should know what is expected of them. From the employees' point of view it is important that clear expectations are articulated. Targets should be provided to allow employees to measure their progress and evaluate the final contribution to the organization. For the organization, the responsibility is to provide clear indication of acceptable levels of performance, timelines and deadlines.

Employees try their utmost to work hard for the organizations, which employ them. They want to have a clear understanding of how they can progress within the organization. They are not interested in rhetorical, generalized platitudes about how they get promoted if they work hard. Clay Carr (1995) stated:

"People do what makes sense to them. If you want them to do their job well for you, make sure that doing it well makes sense and doing it poorly doesn't." [2]

Today's employees are motivated by facts and measurements. They want to know all the avenues opened to them, so that they can make a decision to pursue their goals, within the parameters set by the organization. They want to know the reporting procedures, which will allow them to track their progress. They want to know the bottom line – "if I perform well, what I get?" In reference to this statement, Sloma (1987) wrote:

"I want my competence to be judged solely and exclusively on my performance, not on any other external, extraneous factors."[3]

Although the above statement may sound slightly selfish in a collaborative environment, the statement still holds true. Even individuals within a team or group require a clear understanding of the organization's expectations and the methodology used to evaluate their progress and achievements. Today's knowledge workers want to be able to track and gauge his or her own progress; they want to be able to understand the measure by which their superiors will judge them. Most importantly, in this era of participation, they want to know where they stand in relation to their peers and colleagues. Employees want to know when they will be rewarded for their accomplishments, they also want to know what punishment will be incurred if they do not perform to expected levels.

Motivation is a balance between measurements and control on one hand, and performance and reward/punishment on the other. The former allows management to control and monitor in an effective, fair and consistent manner. The latter, encourages and fosters employee motivation. When these two elements are in congruence, harmony between employee and employer comes to fruition, and productivity and performance becomes the norm. It is therefore important to understand that the more employees can influence their future and behavior; their motivation to achieve will be greater. The requirement is for policies that clearly define the expectations as well as the potential rewards.

Human Resources' Policies

Many of the difficulties faced by today's organizations can be alleviated through good human resources policies and personnel management. For example, careful selection of employees, and the matching of competencies and job descriptions are of paramount importance in motivating employees properly. Inappropriate promotions can have a debilitating effect on staff. Too often people have not been promoted based on their skills and abilities, but rather based on tenure and seniority, especially in unionized organizations. In the age of information and era of knowledge workers, these policies no longer motivate employees. It is not just a question of rewarding employees who have shown diligence or agreed with the hierarchy who should be promoted. Instead those employees who possess the best abilities and competencies should fill positions. Rewarding an employee no longer means that he or she should automatically be promoted to the next step up the ladder. Motivation can be achieved through other rewards, which do not have the potential to upset the delicate interpersonal balance that exists within a group.

In the past, organizations have viewed the person, who arrived early and left late, as a major contributor and hard worker. Often these people were automatically promoted to management. However, working long hours does not necessarily mean that an employee is productive, committed and therefore management material. It could also mean that the employee is perhaps, unorganized and not efficient, hence the long hours. In this new era of technology, it is not long hours alone that should be rewarded; motivation of employees must take into account skills, competencies, overall individual and team contributions including results.

Personnel policies should include specifications for skills and levels of performance required within defined 'job families'. While providing a clear definition of the abilities and skills required for each step of the ladder, it is also important to provide a description for each step in the career ladder. Employees can be rewarded for acquiring and gaining the appropriate skills for the job. It is therefore possible to reward an employee without being promoted to the next step up the ladder to receive a financial reward. This procedure allows the organization to reward employees who are not interested in management while they can still contribute by developing their own specialist skills. In the age of flatter organizations, it is wise to understand that not all employees aspire or are capable to manage, but that their contribution and competencies should nevertheless be rewarded without having to promote them up the ladder. We must also, acknowledge that identification of competence necessitates the proper and objective appraisal of all employees.

Appraisals

Ken Blanchard says that 'feedback is the breakfast of champions'. Can you imagine successful athletes without a coach to indicate their weaknesses or progress and work together on improvements? Why should it be different for employees within an organization that aspires to high performance? Appraisals are therefore important to both the employee and the employer. However, in the context of participative management some adjustments must be undertaken.

In the past, immediate supervisors have done most employee appraisals and in the case of blue collar workers have been practically non-existent. To accomplish proper motivation employees require proper feedback. The old method of Management by Objectives (MBO) has many flaws that make it somewhat redundant in this new era. MBO, in many cases was based on a set of objectives worked out between employee and employer (supervisor), in order to monitor progress and form the basis for evaluation. However, in most cases the objectives were not those of the employee but were rather those of the supervisor. The employee had very little input in the objectives *per se,* his or her objectives were agreed upon to fit the supervisor's objective to accomplish some target or strategy. MBO is not based on proper discussions and employee participation, but is often based on pre-decided strategies and tactics to be complied with by the employee. Much of this type of motivation is based on the principle of the 'carrot and the stick'. The employee is required to perform a set of objectives or be hanged by his or her own petard. Under this regime, at the time of appraisal, it is easy for the supervisor to point out mistakes or achievements and walk out of the process. Usually there was no follow up during the course of the year, and employees were mostly left to their own devise, until the next review.

Today, to properly motivate employees, especially in a collaborative environment, what is required is a new methodology of appraisal. Employees must be given the opportunity to set their objectives based on clearly established strategies, properly communicated by management. The individual or team should be part of the decision-making process, and they should set targets. They must also be part of the evaluation process; members and teams should be subject to peer reviews and assessments. The supervisory appraisal under MBO was too subjective and performed by ill-trained personnel. If rewards are to be allocated based on team and organizational performance then appraisals should be done in the same manner, not by individuals with a subjective point of view. For appraisals to be an effective tool of motivation, it is important that it be fair, inspires trust, is equitable and embraces the same participative concept, which is advocated for the structure of organizations.

Employee Values

Corporate culture which exhorts the organization values and beliefs is the norm in this post era of restructuring and downsizing. However, it seems that once again, the employees' values are being taken for granted or ignored. It is also true to say that some organizations have taken their employees' values and needs into consideration and have used them to great success in motivating their employees. In fact a Fortune Magazine 1998 survey found that:

> "On the principle that it takes many attractions to hold the best, dozens of companies . . . are also generously distributing so-called soft benefits – comforts promoting the elusive work/life balance that is

every bit as important to hard-working employees as the nature of the job itself. . ."[4]

But by and large, many organizations, especially those with large bureaucratic cultures have not really embraced the concept of employee value recognition. It is therefore; fair to mention that more recognition of employees new found values must be taken into consideration for proper motivation.

The development of managers and employees, as a motivational tool, must be undertaken to match the respective needs of the employee and those of the organization. Since the needs of the organization and the employee are interdependent, a collaborative approach to career development is required. Edgar Schein (1978) stated:

> "Both the organisation and the individual within it are dynamic, evolving systems whose needs change because of changing environments and changing internal factors deriving from age, life experiences and family circumstances. The matching of needs is therefore a dynamic process which must be periodically monitored and managed."

In these rapidly changing times, this statement by Schein becomes extremely relevant. The baby boomers see the need for additional family time as well as a desire to pursue their career as well as planned for their retirement. By the same token, employees, battered by the past cannibalization undertaken by corporations, are less loyal to their employers/corporations than to their respective professions. Fostering employee job satisfaction is becoming a greater challenge for companies. The changing climate affects the four areas of job satisfaction, needs and values of employees: security, self-respect, personal growth and independent thinking. Organizations must be cognizant of these negative effects in order to counteract them through proper motivation in order to attract and retain skilled employees.

Career Values & Needs

In today's environment, employees understand that the contract of old that promised "job security and a life-time career with the same corporation," is gone forever. This change, has also affected their values and most importantly their point of view regarding their careers. The knowledge workers of today see themselves as fairly mobile and consider themselves as mercenaries, rather than loyal corporate workers. To this effect, they continuously upgrade their skills to respond to the requirements of an ever-changing work environment. Training and development has become extremely important to today's employees. Organizations who do not provide a learning environment and/or the possibility of further education and development will find it extremely hard to attract skilled workers. Sumantra Goshal, of the London Business School was quoted in an article by the Financial Post:

> "First, recruits need the promise of being trained and developed so as to have permanent option of employment elsewhere. Second, the company needs to ensure the option is exercised at its discretion, not the employees'. It wants a stable and committed workforce that can still be got rid of."

As can be seen the matching of corporation and employee's needs will become more difficult, and new ways to motivate employees become more important. Employers are required to find new ways to motivate and build a sense of commitment in and for their employees. The lure of financial motivation alone is losing its luster, as employees' needs tend to be less materialistic. The battered workforce seeks training and development, time off with the family, leisure and other pursuits. A good example of non-financial reward was used by one of the author's clients: "Remington Energy, a small but very successful Calgary Oil & Gas company, chose to reward a very successful team of four workers in a non-monetary fashion. These young under-forty executives, do very well financially, they have good salaries, stock options, etc. When asked what they would like as a bonus for their accomplishments, their answer was a bike trip in Utah. That's what they got. They spend some time together relaxing and enjoying themselves, and thus reinforcing their bonds."

Many employees want to take part in community activities. For many workers today, the opportunity to enhance their professional status outside of the organization has become priority. Some American companies are responding to these needs. Merck, TRW, Kraft General Foods and Celtech, to name a few, encourage their employees to participate by giving their time to contribute to their profession or favorite charity.

Family Values

While employees' needs and values are changing, one other factor is significantly affecting corporations' outlook on how to motivate their staff. As the children of baby boomers' grow older, there is a resurgence of family values in society. Many workers today, have children in their early teens and younger, and the need to find time for them is becoming a priority and a problem for those families with two working parents. Motivation for these people comes in a different form. They want flextime, time off to spend with their kids, and they look at telecommuting as the means to work. While politicians and society are consistently talking about family values, North American companies are less supportive of these values. Recent reports in *Fortune* show that families are no longer a big plus for a corporation; in fact they seem to have become a big problem. In the restructured corporations, those workers who still have a job are being asked to work longer hours and perform better. The strain on family life is getting harder rather than easier. The promise of more leisure time with the advent of technology has not been fulfilled. Parents have to juggle between career and family. Often working husbands and wives do not see each other for days because they are on the road. In North America 84% of married households, have both the wife and husband working. Children seem to spend more time in day-care or with nannies than they spend with their parents. There is a need for corporations to re-evaluate their approach to young parents. The work constraints have to change in order to help parents have healthy kids, and families, corporations are cognizant of this fact but few are doing something about it, to their own detriment, as reported by Betsy Morris:

> "On some level corporate America know this. Because even if it doesn't much care for families, it surely cares about a brain drain. Companies that don't do more to let parents be parents will begin to lose them. People who want children will find a better way."[7]

The shift in attitude towards work holds true for both men and women. Corporations must find a way to change the male-oriented work pattern which demands long hours of commitment and performance to stay on the promotion ladder. More men are beginning to feel that quality of life is important to them too. Men are gradually pressing for shorter hours. They want flexibility in their work schedules in order to spend more time with their families, and to pursue other non-work related activities.

Although family values are not yet appreciated as a means to motivate employees in the majority of corporations, many others have started to put into place programs that allow workers to be better parents and spend more time with their kids. Many corporations are now introducing day-care facilities on the premises to allow parents of young kids to bring their children to work. Technology is allowing employees to do more work from home. For example, in Washington DC., some government departments have started "telecenters", where employees can go to work closer to home, instead of commuting for up to five hours a day. More corporations are adopting this working environment. The number of 'telecommuters' is increasing at a rapid rate.

Job-sharing is another way that some organizations are instituting to help workers spend more time with their families. Corporations must restructure themselves for flexibility to provide for the needs and values of their employees. This flexibility can also be used to motivate a workforce that increasingly requires flexibility in the work pattern to get closer to their own values, which includes the family, as a major component.

In essence, while companies restructure and formulate new strategies to fit their objectives, goals and their own values, it is important to remember that employees' values are equally important. Individual, as well as family values should take a larger precedence in corporate strategies. The employee/corporate fit is essential for mutual benefits. In an ever-changing work environment it becomes imperative that the atmosphere is congenial for the achievement of goals, and stress should be reduced to a bare minimum.

Reducing Stress

The change faced by today's businesses presents opportunities as well as grounds for disruption and disturbance. As restructuring, downsizing and other strategies are implemented, corporations are consistently raising the levels of stress in their environment. Change, whether positive or negative, causes stress, and the effects are one of the most demotivating factors affecting workers today. Insecurity, dismissals, additional responsibilities, control, and lack of job satisfaction are only a few of the factors increasingly affecting workers. It is key for human resources specialists to be able to identify the symptoms of stress, and advise management about reducing the levels of stress that results in decreasing productivity.

The good news is: change can be used as a motivating factor, (however, it is the steps used to implement change which require a clear understanding). To motivate with empathy requires tact and discipline. The path to successful change should start with careful planning in order to anticipate and tackle foreseeable problems. The organization should foster a culture, which promotes workers' acceptance to take responsibility for their physical and mental health, and help them maintain it.

Undue stress is more commonly caused by the lack of proper communication. Effective communication is the difference between ensuring acceptance and causing damaging resistance in the workforce. To maximize the opportunities which change can bring to an organization, it is important that the human factor takes priority. Innovative personnel policies can bring harmony and maintain motivation in difficult times. These policies should include procedures to minimize stress for those people leaving through dismissals, as well as those employees who stay. Counseling should be provided for all employees affected by change. Groups of individuals or teams can work together to talk about their problems and exchange ideas on dealing with stress. Workshops or counseling sessions of that nature can help to break down barriers and foster stronger links among the survivors of the organization. By promoting and encouraging some of these initiatives dealing with stress and the human factor, personnel staff and departments can improve their profile. They can become a catalyst for managing and motivating staff in very stressful and difficult times.

The upheavals of reengineering have showed us that employees are no longer motivated by financial rewards alone. Increasingly they are reassessing their lives, careers and functions in relation to their contributions to their employers. While employees are trying to adjust to their new work environment, it is also important for corporations to reevaluate their policies regarding the human assets of their organizations. Motivation in this new era of technology and change must undergo severe assessment. Stress has become a major factor in the decline of productivity. It must be reduced in order to recapture enthusiasm in the workforce and gain participation, which in turn will lead to success, and achievement.

Missed Opportunity

On March 17, 1998 the City of Calgary experienced one of the worst snowstorms in a hundred years. In many areas of the city, at least three feet of snow was on the ground, most roads, including major arteries were unusable. The transit system was in no better shape. Under those circumstances a vast majority of Calgarians found it impossible to get out of their house, let alone go to work. The City was at a standstill for at least 24 hours until personal driveways, roads; streets were cleared either by private contractors or public services.

The City of Calgary, largely responsible for the clearing of streets and roads and providing public transportation had many of its employees stranded and unable to come to work like everybody else in the city. However, a week later the City Administrators presented to Council a policy for approval which stated that any employee who did not attend work on the 17th of March 1998 due to the storm, would have to either work overtime during lunch hours or forfeit a day's pay or a day's holiday to make up for their absenteeism. This proposal was accepted and the decision imposed on the employees of the City of Calgary immediately.

Given the nature and purpose for the absenteeism of the majority of employees, and given that only a very small minority of employees actually made it to work, this decision to me, is a clear case of missed opportunity to motivate with empathy. Would it not have been better for the administration to ask Council to approve a day's pay or a day's additional holiday for those workers who made it to work? Would such a gesture be so expensive to the City, that taxpayers would have been outraged? Or was it, once again an assertion of power and control, typical of a bureaucratic organization?

The old 'stick and carrot' methodology of motivation no longer works. Corporations must take employees' values into the motivation and reward equation. 'Time off' for relaxation and with the family must be introduced as a motivating factor. Technology can be used to introduce flextime and other new work patterns in the organization. The objective of motivation should be to increase morale among a battered workforce. Long hours and over-commitment to work does not necessarily mean increased productivity. But happy, less stressed employees produce a workforce who is more committed and add value to the organization through increased productivity. Employees with a clearer sense of their own priorities generally are better prepared to cope with the forces of change, and they are likely to be more successful. Eventually their success contributes to the overall success of the organization, which benefits from their motivation.

Tips for Success

MOTIVATION

Communicate goals and results clearly
Notice and reinforce positive behaviors
Recognize simple things as well as high profile deeds Reward results, instead of effort
Build reward programs for individuals
Offer informal praise then reward formally
Take responsibility for team's mistakes
Review programs regularly to prevent getting stale

Now that we have covered the 'Pillars' of the team concept, it is time for us to focus on the essentials of gaining and maintaining **TRUST**. The next Chapters will concentrate on these issues and provide the basis for these principles. Nothing can be achieved successfully if there is a communication gap. It makes sense that we should start by examining why we should . . .

CHAPTER 11

Transfer Information to get Action

"Competitive people want to know what their company
is trying to excel at."
– Andrall E. Pearson.

"People without information cannot act responsibly. People with
information are compelled to act responsibly."
– Ken Blanchard.

EARLIER WE EMPHASIZED communication or the transfer of information was at the heart of a successful strategy for participative management. In the late 90s often called the beginning of information age era, it is amazing to find that corporations still kept secrets from their employees and stakeholders. Organizations, cannot force employees to be committed to their values, and neither can they control whether employees stay committed to them. However, corporations and other organizations can provide clear, trustworthy, and consistent information, which can help towards the creation of mutual trust. In today's organizations, whether hierarchical or flattened, the layers of management prevent consistent and clear transfer of information. Often, messages from the top get translated along the way and lose their effectiveness. Garbled or fuzzy information can prove to be costly for organizations while problems are investigated and corrected. The use of information to improve work performance is also critical for the understanding of morale, and job satisfaction among employees.

In many companies employees are still taken for granted, and information is still on a 'need to know' basis. These same employees are relied upon for quality, efficiency and performance to match the competition. How can they provide support and performance when they are not properly informed, and are usually the last to know about the company's decisions? As Blanchard, Carlos and Randolph (1996) state:

> "People without information cannot act responsibly. People with information are compelled to act responsibly." [1]

Management has a critical role to play in improving internal communication. One of the qualities sought after in great leaders is that of the great communicator. So why is it that so many workers place the lack of communication as one of the top complaints about management? The rhetoric must stop, and employees must be treated as the valued assets they really are. They should be kept informed in a consistent, clear and honest manner in order to gain their trust and cooperation. It is therefore, imperative for us to examine the different aspects of good communication including the new avenues available to both management and employees to improve communication and the role of management in attaining the objective of open and trustworthy communication.

Include, Exclude through Communication

Employees or any member of an organization are entitled to be informed. They have the right to be included in the basic information channel. Employees have the right to expect to be asked about their ideas and be treated as important assets of the organization. They have the right to be trusted and be given the responsibility to handle the information in a proper manner.

Very often management is afraid of sharing information with employees, especially when it is bad news. Managers try to minimize the issues, sugarcoat and sometimes cloud the message to prevent possible confrontation. Employees are adults, and should be treated as such. Good communication is good business. No matter how bad the news, it should be given in a clear manner. Ideally a question and answer session should be used. Informed employees understand issues better and can be of help in good as well as difficult times. Informed employees are better equipped to deal with adversity, and make contributions to the success of the company, while recognition of their efforts help to raise morale and provide them with self-satisfaction. When employees are presented with the facts, they are usually more receptive to management's message, whether good or bad. Through effective communication management does not entirely remove the pain which comes with bad news, but removes the problems associated with rumors when information is not clearly passed along the line. In their book *The Leading Edge*, Mark Potts and Peter Behr, remind us of the pain of change and how communication can help organizations through the change process.

> "The changes needed to put American companies on the leading edge of the competitive world will not come without pain, but that pain can be minimized through sensitive management and attention to the human details . . . The bottom line for this worker-management partnership, then, is communications. The relationship must be built on a solid, factual understanding about the company's position . . ."

Communication can help ease the pain that is often associated with change. It can be used to explain the reasons to employees, and external parties such as unions, customers and the general media, especially when job loss and closure of factories are part of the bottom line strategies.

Dialogue

In a new collaborative environment, the goal of good communication is to share information between all parties, to resolve conflict, and create better understanding. At its best it promotes teamwork and engenders mutual trust between all parties. At its worst, when communication is not truthful, it creates an atmosphere of mistrust, control, intimidation and fear. Effective communication must be an integral part of the organization's culture. It must be practiced as a three-way traffic flow: top to bottom, upward and lateral.

The old top to bottom transfer of information alone is no longer viable in this era of knowledge workers and information technology. Workers must be treated as responsible channels of information. To strengthen the channels of communication, management must open the doors of communication upward and downward. Employees can only contribute to the success of a company when management listens to their ideas. The so called open-door policy must allow for systems which permit employees to by-pass immediate supervisors – all the way to the CEO if and when necessary without fear of retaliation. Upward communication in hierarchical organization represents the weakest link in most companies. It is important for management to recognize that the values of an open-door culture quickly disappear when autocratic and bureaucratic controls prevent upward communication. Let me share a personal experience: While in the employ of the City of Calgary, I was studying for my MBA, and for my thesis I decided to do a paper on 'Change in the Public Sector'. To perform my research, I required permission to use City of Calgary material, financial data, and conduct an employee survey. Since the Board of Commissioners was the highest level of authority in the hierarchy, I proceeded to request permission directly from The Commissioner of Operations who after discussions and review readily granted me permission to proceed. He immediately provided me with a signed approval, and copies were sent to the respective Department Directors. Two days later, my immediate Supervisor, who had received a copy of the Commissioner's letter from our Director, confronted me. Brandishing the letter she proceeded to question me, not about the paper but about my direct request to the Commissioners, without going through her, **'the proper channel'**."

This example illustrates the problems of upward communication and lack of empowerment. In this case, we were in conflict when the person could not have given me permission in the first place and would have had to go to the Commissioners for approval anyway.

Sometimes, upward communications can be done anonymously, as is the case in some companies. This type of program requires enormous support from the executive suite to prevent any possible loss of face by supervisors, and result in possible retribution. Avie Smith (1991) wrote:

> "To be truly effective, these programs must operate as an adjunct to the chairman's office, with all the prestige and clout this relationship implies. Some organizations have formal upward communication systems that work very effectively with this type of general arrangement: IBM's *Speak Up* is the best known and most emulated. Such programs allow employees to raise questions about company policies and actions-or about how they are treated on the job – and they permit them to do so with complete confidentiality."[3]

When companies make a commitment to good communication that promotes two-way interaction, upward as well as downward, it does not take very long before information starts to flow horizontally. The door for lateral communication is suddenly opened and curbs the culture of segmentalism that may exist in certain organizations. An open system, which allows for the flow of information without restriction, provides an atmosphere of openness that helps workers share ideas and transfer information they receive to other colleagues in all directions. For maximum success the process must work through the organization's structure at least on a daily basis and should be done, if possible, face-to-face. Where breakdowns occur, they should be supplemented by other backup systems that may include brochures, newsletters, and other media, which we shall examine at a later stage. An internal system of open communication must start at the top. Management must assume responsibility and provide support to encourage the information flow and sharing of ideas among every level of the organization and must make communication an essential ingredient of corporate culture.

Management's Role

Good communication starts at the top. Management's role is crucial to the success of any communication system, and should be part of the overall corporate strategy and culture. Clarity and credibility must become the basis of communication in corporations. In the past, management either through caution or misguided public relations strategies has sometimes given the wrong message to its employees and the public at large. When this has happened it has cost the corporation more money to rectify the problem than if the truth had come out in the first place. Accepting blame and taking responsibility is always cheaper in the long run. Truth as a message is supported by numerous incidents. Examples of success and failures can be found in cases such as the Union Carbide tragedy at Bhopal, the Tylenol sabotage incident, BP, Enbridge oil spills, and the tainted blood cases resulting in the transmission of diseases such as HIV, AIDS, etc., in many countries.

If the message is not delivered properly and truthfully the public losses trust in the organization and it can damage the credibility of the institution. Top management in every organization must put into place policies and procedures to create a climate which fulfills their leadership responsibilities. Management should establish a system of on-going channels to deliver messages to its employees and the public. In order to gain the benefits of good communication, all managers and supervisors should be made responsible for the transfer of information. The sharing of ideas across all levels of the organization should be given top priority. The human resource function should include training in communication skills, and should be supported by rewards for good communicators.

Management must understand that the communication function is not only beneficial to performance and increased productivity, but also results in better understanding, trust, job satisfaction and active participation by all employees. It is the duty of management to issue a clear statement of commitment and support for the chosen process of communication. Major business issues should be at the center of employee communication, and openly discussed in various media of communication. Financial support should be provided to keep all channels of communication open and functioning at maximum levels, and the entire system should be subjected to regular evaluation to maintain its integrity and efficiency.

Media

There are several means of communication available to organizations to inform both their internal and external public. While the grapevine is a great source of information, it can also carry rumors, which may not be good for the overall transfer of information. This basic form of communication should be complemented by a more structured system. It is worthwhile to spend some time discussing some of these channels of information and their usage.

Face-to-face

Nothing beats the direct interaction between employer and employee. It can be done at any level and at any time. While the formal use of regular meetings between employees and their supervisors are usually the norm in corporations, other types of meetings should not be ignored. Employees should be encouraged to hold meetings among themselves without supervisors to discuss their concerns and tasks' performance. Visits by senior members of staff to offices or factories should be organized. Regular meetings between union representatives and management should take place to keep each other informed. All structured meetings should be conveyed to all parties involved, and newsletters and bulletins can be used effectively for this purpose.

Interaction among all employees should be encouraged. The conversations at the water cooler are often the source of great ideas and provide a useful means of information transfer. Walking around and asking employees for their ideas and their thoughts are often a great source of information. It is also a very inexpensive way of feeling the pulse of the working force. Information gathering in this manner is not scientific, but provides a valuable insight into employee opinions and should be part of a corporations' overall communication strategy. Through this process barriers between levels of the hierarchy may also disappear. In my 1994 dissertation *'Change in the Public Sector'* I provided the following example:

> "Some years ago, Richard Picherak, City Manager(CM) of the City of Edmonton, put into place some interesting communication systems. He had a monthly 'brown bag lunch' where every employee was invited to talk and participate in an exchange of ideas with the CM during the lunch hour. The Mayor and the CM also went out in the field to talk to employees on a regular basis. Richard Picherak felt that the use of informal channels helped him communicate more openly with the City's staff. One of the results of this system was the acquisition of the right equipment, because front line employees were encouraged to talk directly to the CM".[4]

Newsletters

An effective way of communicating is through a regular newsletter, which provides information about the corporation's issues, as well as personal employee information. However, it must not be done in such a way as to be filled with too much employee trivia such as, birthdays, and anniversaries and sports achievements. Similarly it must not become the 'house-organ' where every bit of information is seen as pandering to management's pronouncements, egos and good deeds. This type of communication is unproductive and can be seen as cynical, and in that case it does not serve any useful purpose.

Good information in a bulletin or newsletter should contain material, which focuses on serious corporate challenges, values, plans and goals. Employee work performance and community achievements should be highlighted and given its proper place in the context of corporate goals. Although some companies have experimented with joint publications involving Unions, I do not support this form of communication. In many cases it may harden the perception of propaganda by management or unions and decrease objectivity and credibility of the information given to employees. However, the publication may suffer political problems and disappear as a result of disagreement between the publishers. The quality of the publication should be high in order to give it respect and credibility. The information should be frequent, at least on a monthly basis – anything less will minimize its importance. Corporate publications should preferably be mailed to the employees' homes where they have more time to spend reading it. It also extends readership to family members and provides respect for the publication.

Television and Video

The proliferation of a multitude of media makes it easier to communicate, both internally and externally. TV, Video Tapes and Video Conferencing have become a great enhancement to communication. The first two, provide a means of direct communication but is only one way. The increase affordability of Video conferencing on the other hand has opened the door for two-way communication over long distances.

TV and videotapes are used to inform and train employees. Increasingly, large companies with operations in many different locations use video tapes as a consistent means of communication. While training through videotapes seems to be catching on, it still does not replace the immediate interaction provided through face-to-face training. Also, there are small drawbacks to the use of videotapes. They are expensive to produce, and they result in increased production time costs when employees are taken off the job to watch them.

Teleconferencing on the other hand is being used more often. Meetings of managers and conference between employees from different locations are being conducted in this manner. The exchange of ideas between employees working far apart is being facilitated through this technology. Through the use of personal computers, conferencing face to face is also being used as an effective communication medium. Due to greater competition in the communication industry, cost is no longer a major obstacle to the proliferation of teleconferencing.

Internet/Intranet

As information technology improves, virtually on a daily basis, the excuses not to communicate become more redundant. The proper use of the appropriate medium can increase the flexibility of the organization's communication system, and allow access to a wider audience. The proliferation of the Internet has provided companies with a new medium of communication, which seems to be borderless and without restrictions. Cyberspace has provided companies, governments and individuals an enormous billboard to inform the world about virtually everything. Advertising and communication with the general public has become much easier. The number of World Wide Web sites is growing at an enormous rate. As e-commerce increases, small businesses can compete against corporate giants by operating on the Internet. They can advertise their products and services and reach a wider audience. Information about products and services are being posted on the net to inform the market about current availability and future developments.

Similarly, companies are using an internal system comparable to the Internet to communicate with employees. The intranet is company specific and allows employees to communicate across levels of the organization. The sharing of ideas and access to company information is virtually instantaneous. It has the potential of cutting paper and increase the sharing of ideas. At Nestlé, it is often said that the intranet allows communication between the worldwide units in a free and unfettered environment. An increasing number of companies are even using the Intranet to process orders, set up warehouse receipts, shipping labels etc. Then there is the potential of linking intranets and web sites between companies to conduct business known as B2B. Intranets make financial sense because they exist as services with minimal hardware costs as they use existing corporate servers, workstations and PCs. Looking ahead, the use of largely free Internet technology, availability of circuits and broadband, low costs and large potential payoffs will see more firms build intranets and links.

The nagging problems will become the management of information and security. Not to worry, already there exists programs which ensure that employees do not waste time surfing for irrelevant material and there are 'firewalls' already in place to maintain security for highly classified material. In short, the internet will open new avenues of communication, both internally and externally. The increased use of intranets in organizations will further help to better manage teams and allow the flow of information across boundaries never crossed before. The objective is to allow the users to manage the information. The answer is to allow access to relevant information and manage the security of the network at the same time.

Surveys & Employee Suggestion Programs

To encourage employee participation and enhance communication channels, two additional initiatives can be put to effective use.

Surveys are a great vehicle to gather employee reaction to management policies and strategies. When conducting surveys it is essential that the questionnaire be designed properly. Structured questions will result in quantitative data which can be essential to the company, while a couple of open-ended questions will provide straight from the heart expressions from employees. It is a great vehicle for upward communication with management. Confidentiality and shielding of identity is a prerequisite for surveys to be effective as only under these circumstances will management get candid and honest answers to their questions.

Employee suggestion programs are another way to promote upward communication. Properly administered programs can result in substantial savings for the company. Any such program should be backed by proper evaluation and with a prompt reward system. For years, Japanese companies have been using suggestions programs to make themselves more competitive. In their case they concentrate on small continuous improvements based on the philosophy of "*Kaizen*", thus gaining large number of small suggestions from a great number of employees. By contrast the Western approach has been to focus on large savings that do not really focus on employee involvement. No matter which method is used, an employee suggestions program, which encourages better communication, is better than nothing at all.

Telecommuting

As the number of stay-at-home workers increases, communication and transfer of information will have to improve. Telecommuters generally are knowledge workers who are independent and require minimal supervision. However, to perform their tasks they will require clear, detailed and specific information. Their supervisors, who may be miles away, will have to develop new communications skills to provide them with information. Corporations will have to establish appropriate telecommuting models to allow employees to be productive. High Tech companies such as Cisco Systems of California, already use sophisticated systems to allow their employees to communicate with headquarters. Employees have installed ISDN connections, fax/printers and are equipped with Pentium Notebooks and Palm equipment, which they can take on the road and communicate with headquarters at any time from virtually anywhere. In addition, e-mail has become a major factor in this new information age. By using e-mail telecommuters and even traditional office workers can communicate with each other, or the world for that matter, cheaply, efficiently and quickly. Today with have more tools of communication through the social media which includes Twitter and Facebook.

Reports

Autocratic and bureaucratic organizations jealously protect information because they sincerely believe that it provides them with maximum power. These organizations forget that knowledge achieves power only when it is shared with the people who can make it work – the workers. In many organizations it is very difficult for management to share information once believed to be confidential. Managers of these organizations have a philosophy, which prevents them from sharing information that is not detrimental to the company. Fortunately, this situation is changing.

Many companies today are sharing information with their employees, because they have found that sharing promotes participation. Information, formerly classified as confidential are now being released to employees for information purposes. Data such as costing results, variance analysis, quality defects or tolerance measures, comparisons of actual to budgeted quarterly results, absenteeism, etc., are now part of regular information releases to employees. For example, Jaclyn Fierman (1995) reports about SRC, a subsidiary of former International Harvester in those terms:

> "Each week the company shuts down the machines for half an hour while its 800 employees break into small groups to study the latest financial statements. The workers have more than a passing curiosity in the numbers: Last year SRC distributed $1.4 million in bonuses pegged to how each division performed against line items like profit before taxes."[5]

Reports in the form of hard copies can be made available to employees and their Supervisors. Some companies have computer monitors in specific shop floor locations where employees can have access to performance data. Regular meetings of teams, quality circles and group of employees are held to discuss the latest results and evaluate performance. An example of increased employee participation through availability of reports is provided by the City of Calgary – Waterworks program as I illustrated (1994):

> "In the early eighties The Transmission & Distribution Division of the City of Calgary – Waterworks, was experiencing annual loses of approximately $2 million. Through quality circles involving every worker in the division, union and non-union, much inefficiency was identified and changes were made. The Accounting staff in collaboration

with operating employees designed a new unit cost system. Proper variance analysis reports were designed to communicate results to each level concerned. Significant in-roads were made in processes, productivity and most of all, worker participation. In the first year alone, there was a $2 million surplus. This achievement was published and recognized in 1986, by a National Productivity Award of Excellence from the Canadian Society of Industrial Engineer's."[6]

Shared information is part of the continuous improvement process. The Japanese, have shown us, how continuous improvement through *Kaizen* have made their products so competitive. Employees are provided information as a means to evaluate their performance. A steady diet of relevant information contributes to their understanding of how they are doing against the competition. When they are aware of their performance only then can they contribute, make improvements, and suggest new ideas to increase productivity or efficiency. The main goal is to encourage employee participation; however we should also be cognizant of possible obstacles.

Barriers to Good Communication

In general, most managers acknowledge the importance of good communication. In reality, there are barriers to good communication that should not be ignored. Resistance to change is always a major barrier to any progressive strategy, and open communication is not immune to it. Obstacles come in different forms and they may be found in all types of organizations, but very often they are not recognized as a problem by management. In order to improve communication we shall look at these obstacles and provide some solutions to the problem.

Managerial Support

Very few organizations or their top management will accept that communication is not their top priority. Yet when their corporate culture is looked at closely barriers to communication can be seen to abound. The support required is not only financial but requires a deep understanding that good communication is a critical factor in gaining employees' trust and commitment. Providing the necessary staff and budgets is not the only solution, but the support required involves management to 'walk the talk' by being more open and inclusive through their actions.

Autocratic, bureaucratic rules and culture inhibit good communication. Often the pretext of confidentiality is used to prevent the decimation of information. Of course there is always information that is of a classified nature. However, workers are not really interested in that type of information anyway. Employees require information that affects them personally, information about their work and their performance, their contribution to the bottom line and the sharing of ideas. Too often, management does not trust its employees and therefore establish complicated approval systems and restrict or confine information to certain levels of the organization.

Communication in most companies is still based on a 'need to know' basis. But these same organizations will seek greater worker participation. Many managers guard information jealously as a source of asserting and maintaining power. They still believe that the more information they have and the less information is given to lower levels of staff, provides them with control. In order to open the doors of communication, top executives must break down the barriers and hierarchies that prevent good communication. Managers must be given the authority and ability to transfer information to employees when needed. Information should not be restricted to supervisory levels alone. Relevant data should be available to the people who are responsible for implementing and performing tasks. Very often to obfuscate the issue management resorts to using long-winded and rampant prose to communicate.

Bureaucratese

The use of many words where only a few can explain the issue, or the use of bizarre terms to conceal the truth is termed 'bureaucratese'. This form of communication is prevalent in the public sector and has found its way into the private sector. To mask or dress up a communiqué, the communicator resorts to the use of obscure forms of dissemination of information. The words used, in that case, are so convoluted that they can take a fairy-tale meaning while not giving direct or right information. An example from Prose-Busters Communications illustrates this very well:

They said: "It should be possible to effect definitive identification."
What they meant: "You should know who you're dealing with."

The problem with this kind of communication is that it is not only counterproductive, but also expensive. The reasons for its existence are that certain communicators choose to create ambiguity which will in turn give them the power to make the necessary interpretation, as and when they see fit. The use of bureaucratese, is often the cause of malaise in the workplace and is a major factor for mistrust of government and large corporations.

The Truth Complex

Reasons for not communicating abound, the fear of telling the truth is very often the root cause of the problem, because most organizations suffer from a truth complex. There are certain deeply rooted managerial beliefs which often prevent the communication of bad news. Management often believes that employees cannot handle negative news that they are not capable of balancing the pros and cons to arrive at a reasonable conclusion. Executives are often afraid that employees cannot be trusted with negative information, and that the competition, the media and stakeholders may be made aware of the truth. Interestingly enough, these same Executives will ultimately call a press conference to inform the media about the firm's problems.

These fears and beliefs are totally out of place in today's world. Employees are more knowledgeable, better educated and honestly have the success of their company at heart. It is only management's mistrust which fuels employee dissatisfaction. Employees today would like the facts as they truly are no fudging or camouflage. If the news is negative they want it now, not at the eleventh hour when they cannot plan or make an informed suggestion or contribution. Most of the time, when there is some bad news in the air, the grapevine is already in action.

Today, with the internet and e-mail, and the social media news travels very fast. Any delay by management fuels the rumor mill and creates more uncertainty and fear among employees, suppliers and customers. The lack of communication and the truth complex are often the major causes for media interference and decimation of negative information in the press.

Solutions

The solutions to communications problems can be found in the corporate culture. Executives must make a serious effort to change the culture which prevents or/and inhibits the transfer of information. Information should be made to work for the organization, and the old beliefs of confidentiality must be removed in order to create an open climate where workers are encouraged to participate in the decision making process. The sharing of information is a key to continuous improvement. Management does not always have all the answers for improvement. The reality is that improvement lies with the people on the front-line. When workers are given information about their performance, failures to attain targets and their contribution to the bottom line, they are more likely to participate actively in the improvement of the company. Continuous improvement and change are closely related. While change can involve drastic measures, continuous improvement usually involves incremental steps, sometimes one at a time. Nevertheless, change big or small requires good communication.

To facilitate the change process people should be kept informed. All the facts should be made available; the communications should be clear, transparent and devoid of bureaucratese. It is easier to reach consensus and agreement if everybody is in possession of the same facts. To get people to buy-into the needed change, ownership must be encouraged. Ken Blanchard illustrates this better (1997):

> "If you want everyone to have an ownership stake in the change process you must expose them to all the available information"[7]

Organizations who continue to believe that information is power and that confidentiality is a fundamental element of success are deluding themselves. The politics of power and control of information hurt progress. The distribution of information opens many doors to success, accomplishment and recognition. Upward, as well as downward communication channels must be encouraged.

Tips for Success

BETTER COMMUNICATION

Give information to increase involvement
Become visible and accessible
It is not quantity, but clarity that matters
Avoid the use of 'bureaucratese'
Communication is a 'three-way' traffic, top to bottom, bottom-up and lateral
Encourage use of information for continuous improvement
Be honest with good and bad news
Use technology for greater and better communication

We must recognize that management does not always have all the answers, and that employees do have ideas worth of consideration. Contradictory opinions from employees must not be feared or ignored. Too often many good ideas may be discarded because the suggestion may be contrary to company policy. Information availability and sharing is at the core of any improvement process. Employees must be given the information they need to make decisions, which involve their work. It is management's responsibility to encourage employees to be part of the solution by keeping them informed. Information transfer elicits contribution from workers. Employees' ideas and performance, which results in profits and increased market share, can be used as a trampoline to foster collaboration in the organization. Therefore, employees' efforts should always be . . .

CHAPTER 12

Rewarded Equitably

"Things that get recognized and rewarded get repeated."
– Michael Leboeuf.

TODAY'S BUSINESS WORLD is so competitive that organizations are constantly changing to adapt and keep up with events affecting them. New organizational structures, new management concepts, new competencies, and different behaviors are gradually being adopted and accepted in organizations around the world. In order to survive in this competitive environment, companies must acquire speed, improve the quality of their goods and services, and must control and keep costs down.

One of the major costs of a company is labor. In the recent past, to control the cost of labor companies have resorted to restructuring and laying off large number of workers. The socioeconomic impact has been felt in most, if not all industrialized countries. In the past thirty years, North American economic growth has been a result of an increase in the work force rather than real productivity increases. However, in economic terms to keep growth in real income, we require increases in productivity. In North America, most specifically Canada, productivity has not matched high wages and many industries have lost their competitiveness. In addition, a global economy has added to the woes of unskilled workers with relatively high pay. As a result, these workers have been laid off and in some cases many of them do not have the skills required to be re-employed. Middle managers have not escaped this race towards cost effectiveness they too have been downsized.

To rectify this problem requires changes in attitudes, strategies, and approaches to the way we work and how we are rewarded. Unfortunately old organization designs do not fit very well with current business realities. We require a participative solution were workers and organizations get together to work on a new design for the sharing of responsibilities for overall success of the organization, and of course for equitable rewards.

This Chapter attempts to address the difficulties of continuing with existing reward systems in a new environment. A basic factor for the effective functioning of an organization lies in its reward and pay system. While many companies have made successful changes to their administration of rewards in general, changes in reward and pay systems have encountered enormous resistance. More specifically resistance has been very strong in organizations with unionized staff and in the public sector.

Before change is advocated, let us examine the old reward methods under which most existing organizations operate. As we change the way we work and the manner in which organizations function we require new approaches to pay and rewards. If organizations are restructuring in the pursuit of high performance and high productivity, the reward system should match those goals. I shall look at some ideas and new approaches towards pay systems, which address new organizational realities.

The strategic agenda of an organization should be the starting point for the design of any reward system. Since it is believed that the new strategy should be one of participation, effective participative management also means that it is time to look at participative designs for team appraisals and rewards. As we move towards hiring for competencies, we should also look at rewarding employees for their specific competencies. In effect I put forward ideas for an overhaul of pay systems to better reflect the new business environment.

To provide flexibility and better cost control I propose that pay strategies should be restructured to include a three-tier system comprised of a base pay, a bonus or performance component and a benefits package. To address the issue of equitable pay we shall also look at the rewards of executives – how their remuneration are arrived at and why some concepts can and should equally be applied to employees' rewards. The objective is to promote a pay and reward system, which reflects the strategies of the organization while it truly motivates employees towards higher performance levels.

Rewards as a Motivator

Organizations have used rewards and pay systems to attract and retain competent staff. But one of the most important aspects of rewards has been as a motivator and the vast majority of research on this subject supports the point of view that rewards have a strong impact on motivation. However, the other side of the debate about motivation addresses the issue of how different rewards affect different employees. The argument revolves around whether job satisfaction or money is the determining factor for motivation. Since motivation was addressed earlier, here I shall focus on the monetary aspect only.

Although money is always mentioned as a powerful tool of motivation, it is not always easy to design a reward system, which will motivate performance. One of the difficulties encountered is the measurement of performance. Measurements can be established for the individual, for a group, or even for the organization, but none is better than the others. The fact is that for a reward to be meaningful and effective it must be of some value to the recipient. Pay in most circumstances seems to be the reward of choice; it either provides status or provides the basis for the acquisitions of things that can provide another form of reward. Other rewards such as job satisfaction or a larger office, for example, may provide another type of value. In one-way or another to be successful the reward must fulfill the employee's needs.

The reward must produce some form of excitement. This is why an annual 2% increase is not as exciting as a 10% increase; therefore it is very likely that the 2% raise may not be a great motivator. Although people differ in many ways, for the reward to have an impact it is best that it be credible and that it can be influenced by the recipient. The latter is very important, because it provides the individual with the ability to influence his/her performance through changes in behavior. The more publicity the reward receives, the better the value derived from it. Edward E. Lawler III(1990) stated:

> "For example, rewards that are in the public domain tend to be valued much more than those that are not. The reason for this is simple: rewards in the public domain have much more status value than do rewards that are secret. It is hard for people to receive acknowledgments from others if their good performance and rewards are secret."

The other aspect of reward as a motivator is its measurement. Performance can be measured by the traditional appraisal system which tends to be subjective, or it can be measured through financial results as is the case for determining executives' bonuses. As the business environment undergoes drastic changes, it is time for the measurements used to determine rewards in this new era, to undergo similar changes. Since participation and teamwork is proposed as a means to drive the new environment, it stands to reason that rewards should also be designed as a collective effort, and that the measurement of performance should be driven by the strategic objectives of the organization. Prior to looking at new ways of determining rewards and designing a system, we should examine the traditional system, which has been used by organizations.

Old Pay System

The bureaucratic model used by most organizations has been the driving force behind the design of existing pay systems. It is based on the assumptions that most people are willing to take orders, and the effectiveness of a hierarchical approach, which promotes a control-oriented style of management. The pyramid is usually made of three levels:

1. The executive level conceptualizes and directs the activities of the organization.
2. The middle managers are entrusted with the task of implementing the strategies and controlling people at a lower level.
3. The third level is assigned carefully prescribed tasks, which requires no problem solving ability. They are required to perform consistently and conscientiously, very often without too much use of their intellectual capabilities.

It follows that under this system; the executives would be paid extremely well because of their level of responsibility. The middle management level would also be compensated quite well because they manage large numbers of people and have the responsibility for seemingly large budgets. The third level in the industrialized world is also well paid, although their abilities to plan, think for themselves and solve problems are underutilized. Similar jobs in the developing world are paid at a relatively low rate. However, in industrialized countries, these workers are paid high wages because there are minimum-wage laws and most of them are members of active unions who, on their behalf, bargain for high wage rates. Over the years wage rates in many industries have risen consistently, to the point where they are no longer competitive with wages in developing countries.

In the past the high costs of labor was not a major factor, because the goods produced in the industrialized world could not be manufactured elsewhere. However, as globalization takes place, more and more developing countries have been able to compete with industrialized countries on labor costs and productivity.

The problem does not only lie in hourly rates, but most other compensation costs are out of line with those of foreign competitors. Much of the traditional pay system is based on fixed costs, made up of salaries/wages and benefits. There are no variable rewards in traditional pay systems. When increases in pay are made, the whole package is affected. Therefore, to keep costs down and increase productivity, organizations usually resort to technology improvements and/or layoffs.

In Japan for example, the pay system is different. They use a low base pay, supplemented by large bonuses, which are based on productivity and profits. This gives the flexibility to reduce labor costs in bad economic times, and prevents massive layoffs that are endemic in western industrialized economies.

Another problem with traditional pay systems is that it is not a motivator. In bureaucratic systems, where traditional pay is prevalent, most salaries and wages are based on clearly defined job descriptions and do not take into consideration any individual or group contribution. In most cases, no matter what the performance level, an employee receives an increase as bargained for by the unions. For management personnel, often their increases are based on performance appraisals, which are done by immediate supervisors, who are often subjective and unskilled in appraisal procedures. To avoid confrontation, many non-union employees receive pay raises without a proper performance appraisal. In this case, tenure and seniority often takes precedence over meritocracy and performance. In addition merit pay is often considered to be an entitlement by workers. Therefore, having achieved entitlement status, merit pay increases with age and tenure. As the working population approaches the age of 55, merit pay will increase, thus augmenting labor costs. The traditional pay system operated by large organizations contributes to the ever-increasing cost of labor and does not provide any incentives to improve productivity. This system creates a vicious circle of high labor costs, no motivation for improvement, underutilized workforce, and eventually, in economic downturns lead to massive layoffs, resulting in socio-economic problems.

To reflect the realities of today's competitive business world, it is time to review the existing traditional system of reward. The loss of competitiveness requires that new approaches to pay are required. As strategies and organizational structures change, alternative pay systems that take into account worker participation, organization's strategic goals and results evaluated through performance measurements must be considered.

New Pay

Traditionally, compensation strategies consist of a base pay designed to attract, motivate and retain employees. They include payment for skills based on specific job descriptions, reward based on performance appraisal and a comparative rate based on similar jobs in other organizations of a similar nature. In addition benefits and bonuses have usually been awarded as a percentage of this base pay. Increases in base pay are cumulative and cause substantial increases in benefits, resulting in the very high cost of labor.

In order to reward employees equitably and achieve organizational strategic goals, an alternative pay system should be looked at. Let us look at an alternative. **New Pay**[2] was first introduced by Lawler (1986) to explain reward programs, which would reflect an understanding of organizational culture, goals, values of a new era of competitiveness and a global economy. The new system, as mentioned earlier, should be made up of three components: Base Pay, Variable Pay and Benefits.

Base Pay

The function of base pay should be to provide employees with an economic reward based on the organization's needs for the skills and competencies required to fill a job, and to reflect the realities of the external market. Since one of the objectives is to encourage improvement and growth, base pay can be used to reward employees who acquire new skills and competencies. In addition base pay can be adjusted to respond to the economics of the external market when certain jobs and/or skills become more or less expensive. As we move to flatter organizations with increasing use of teams, this type of pay makes better sense. This system can still reward people for their skills, responsibilities and competencies without having to move them up the career ladder and allows for both horizontal and vertical career growth. According to Schuster and Zingheim (1992):

> "Where organizations are genuinely interested in improving human resource performance, base pay programs best accomplish the following goals:
> - reflect changes in the economics of the labor markets in which the organization elects to compete for talent
> - serve as the foundation for variable pay
> - reflect either the economic, market, or strategic value of jobs (or the skills required to perform jobs)" [3]

Variable Pay

The second tier of the new pay system is where the gains and flexibility are achieved. Variable pay is used to recognize organizational performance, group and team achievements and is based on the financial ability of the organization to pay. Since variable pay is reassessed periodically, it does not have the compounding effect of an annuity. It is paid when it is earned and is effective for the year in which the performance was achieved. This method of pay is very much in tune with the participative management concept.

Performance is measured in groups and there is a definite sharing of the rewards between the organization and its employees. As the organization succeeds, so do the employees. In times when there are no significant gains, no variable pay is awarded or it is very small. Since variable pay does not become a permanent cost to the employer, it is easier to control the cost of benefits, which are usually based on the fixed portion of direct pay. It also helps in bad economic times, when the variable can be reduced to avoid employee layoff or base pay cuts.

The advantages of a variable pay component within a compensation package are numerous. This system not only promotes partnerships between the organization and the employees, but also encourages team or group accomplishments. It can also help to change corporate culture, foster teamwork and implement customer focused strategies supported by bonuses included in variable pay. Adaptation to a new, more competitive environment will enable variable pay to become more widespread and acceptable and will help forge a closer link between organizations and employees.

Variable pay is a natural tool to reward quality. It can make use of both qualitative and quantitative measurements to foster collaborative behavior. Since it is renewed annually it can be used to match the needs and strategies of the organization as dictated by changing circumstances. In a sense, this component can become the bond between the organization and its workers for a collaborative work environment.

Benefits

It is a well-accepted fact, in certain countries, that organizations should help their employees provide for their health and welfare. Other ones, such as paid time off, disability protection, life insurance and pension funds, sometimes supplement these benefits. However, one of the problems that most organizations face is the increased cost of those benefits.

There are two main reasons for these increased costs. The first one is the simple economic fact that most health care and welfare costs are rising due to changes in the delivery and the higher costs of drugs, facilities etc. The other factor is directly related to the methodology used in the provision of benefits. In traditional compensation agreements, benefits are often a direct percentage of the salary or wage. In this case, as the beneficiary gets an increase in pay, the organization incurs an increase in costs related to its contribution to the benefits component.

Understandably health care, and other benefits are important to employees, but we must also face the fact that it is a very costly to organizations. In order to minimize those costs and still provide good benefits to employees, there must be some compromise and collaboration between employees and organizations to minimize the ever-rising costs of benefits. There are many opportunities for organizations to maintain the provision of good levels of health care and benefits, while making sure that they stay cost effective.

Other benefits such as paid time off, vacations, pensions, and sick leave should also be looked at. These other benefits are also costly and should be taken into account when restructuring the compensation package. Flexibility should become a major objective in the management of these benefits. None of these benefits should reward employees to stay away from work, but could instead be used to forge a better employee-organization partnership.

Strategies involving shared responsibility for these benefits are suggested. In the case of health and welfare benefits, the organization can agree to pay for 'core benefits' which could be based on the wage and salary level, while any additional benefits can be purchased by the employee to suit his or her needs. The organization can negotiate, on behalf of its employees, with carriers of these benefits for cheaper rates under group purchase agreements. In this area, governments will have to make a serious effort to foster a more participative strategy for the management of benefits. While it is commendable for government policies to dictate the importance of organizations to provide certain benefits, it is also time to look at alternative ways, which attempt to provide benefits and manage costs more effectively at the same time. A relaxation in government intervention on this issue will provide organizations with the flexibility to provide certain core benefits, and provide the employees with a choice to complement their particular needs. The role of government on this issue is to ensure that organizations, through credit tax policies, are encouraged to provide benefits because they are effective, and have a positive impact on organizational performance.

Executive Compensation

In order to reward employees more equitably, it is necessary to look at executive compensations, evaluate their structure and the affect on the morale of employees as well as the contribution to the performance of the organization. Before anyone jumps on the bandwagon that this discussion is an attack on executive pay, it is not. But it is rather a look at executive compensation because there are certain elements that can be adopted to reform employees reward systems, and at the same time expose some of the excesses of some executives' compensation.

Traditionally, executives' pay has been a mixture of base pay, plus incentive pay made up of such components as stock options, profit sharing, etc. While the total compensation package for executives was designed to provide an incentive to increase organizational performance, the size of these packages in times of a recession or economic downturn has gradually become the focus of stockholders, unions and minority shareholders' groups. In the recent past numerous examples in North America have shown that certain executive pay levels were not related to how badly or how well their organization had performed. Recently, negotiated severance packages worth millions have also been scrutinized. In effect executive compensation is becoming an issue in some industrialized countries, but most specifically in North America where the disparity between executive and employee compensation is gradually getting larger.

The *Wall Street Journal* reported that in 1995, the Japanese CEO made approximately 32 times the average worker's wages, while the US CEO, made 130 times the average worker's wages.

In June 1996, Danielle Herubin of *The Palm Beach Post* reported that in 1995, while Appletree Cos., lost $12.98 millions on sales of $30 millions, the two company executives got an average increase of 81%.

The two examples above are perhaps a reason why employees and even shareholders are getting skeptical of the management concepts in use in North American companies. More recently, even after the massive collapse of the banking industry, many executives in the United States were reportedly being paid millions in compensation, despite their proven failures. It is not to say that some executives have not deserved their share of reward, but in many cases it has been the size of the compensation, rather than the concept that has been under attack.

While their workers have been laid off, many executives have raised their compensation disproportionately. The double standard has not been totally ignored. In Canada, small groups of shareholders have questioned executives' compensation. There may not be too many successful attempts at reducing the level of executive compensation but these attacks have certainly brought the issue into the open. As corporate governance and ethical values become more important issues for shareholders, compensation is bound to top the list of shareholders' complaints. As reported by the *Globe & Mail*, with reference to the Royal Bank of Canada:

> "One more result of the issues raised by Mr. Michaud, which included an effort to cap CEO compensation at 20 times the average bank salary: It can safely be predicted that no bank board in Canada will ever again award a 50-per-cent increase in the pay of its CEO. That is just too much like trying to install a television antenna in a lightning storm."[4]

Getting Off the Gravy Train

Many companies have used their stocks to acquire companies. Similarly, companies are using stock options to hire and retain senior executives. This reward strategy is associated with the idea that company officers should have some of their wealth linked to risk-taking and results. However, factors such as an increasing bull market has highlighted the deficiencies associated with the use of stock options as a means of rewarding executives. Too many executives, especially in North America, have received double-digit pay raises that were not necessarily based on company performance. While options are not shown on the income statement it is surely an expense, which cannot be ignored. No wonder many stock market analysts have sounded the alarm about the affect of stock options on the distortion of true earnings in companies that freely grant them. However you look at them options are major transfers of wealth from shareholders to management. It is therefore relevant that any compensation program, which includes options, should be reviewed to make them more equitable. What is required is the replacement of current agreements by more stringent ones that will prevent the erosion of wealth and truly reflect pay-for-performance.

The alternatives could include the adoption of plans, which demand that executives provide shareholders with a minimum return on their investment before their options can be exercised. To date, too many executives have benefited from stock options even when their companies have suffered large losses. The new agreements must include genuine risk-related reward pay systems such as those being experimented by some companies. These are some examples:

Performance Vesting: Directors set a short term in which the stock has a chance to rise, and a very high target price. If the stock has not reached its target price within the set time, the executive must forfeit all the options.

Indexed Options: Should the stock increase at the same rate as the S&P 500 the executive gets nothing.

Deferred Bonus: Executives' bonuses are available in 'deferred share units', which are only redeemable upon retirement from the company.

Premium-priced Options: A high target price for the stock is again set. However executives can only keep the gain above the set price.

These are some of the new stock option agreements which have been used to better reflect pay-for-performance and stop wealth erosion in some companies. The best thing about these proposed reforms is that it will reduce the abuse of stock options as a means of rewarding mediocre performances by some executives. It will also remove the antagonism, between rank and file employees and the executive suites, created by this disparity in the reward system.

There is much to be said for the structure of executive compensation. The link of bonuses, such as share options etc., with organizational performance is particularly interesting. This aspect of executive compensation, albeit a reformed one, should be introduced in a proposed restructuring of compensation for workers. Negotiations and discussions should be entertained to get workers on board for a pay-for-performance element within the total compensation package. Increasingly companies in the hi-tech industry extend the use of stock options to both their executives and their employees. What is good for the executive suite should also be good for the rest of the organization's employees.

Participative Management

In order to introduce equity in organizational compensation, there should first be an element of participative management to ensure success. In the first place the good intentions of employees alone are not enough to make a pay-for-performance (PFP) system work. What is required is a blend of people working together, smarter, harder, effectively and within an environment, which promotes the sharing ideas. In the second instance, since profit sharing and gain sharing plans involve collective performance, any accepted formula should provide employees with the ability to influence their behavior and efforts in relation to their bonuses in order to provide proper motivation.

Profit sharing and gain sharing differ slightly. Profit sharing is usually based on the overall financial performance of the organization. Gain sharing on the other hand is closely based on measurements, which do not include all operating costs of the business. It relates more to employee performance as measured against set measurements that usually are within the employees' control. These differences do not mean that these formulae for (PFP) cannot be adapted for specific circumstances. In addition to these two methods, some organizations may choose to include employee ownership. Of course, while employee ownership may not apply to the public sector environment, they can find other means to compensate their employees. Whichever, method of compensation is chosen, there are certain elements that must be present to ensure its success.

In the first place there must be worker participation in the process. Whether an expert is used to introduce the system, it is well advised that a task force is best to bring the issue forward. The use of a task force made up of employees from all levels of the organization is certainly better that the top down approach. This method is more likely to ensure acceptance and trust in the plan.

Any plan must contain comprehensive measurements that can be clearly understood by all employees. In manufacturing surroundings, measurements are easier than in a service environment; nevertheless two elements must be present. Measurements must include factors for both productivity and quality, for it is important that an organization focuses on all its areas of performance. The bottom line is not always the only target, but an equitable compensation system based on performance must be designed to provide flexibility and credibility.

There is a strong belief that any formula used to implement a (PFP) compensation system, requires strong involvement opportunities for employees to influence the measurements used to calculate their bonuses. Employees must be given the opportunity to influence decisions pertaining to operations, costs of material, supplies, inventory management etc. With this in mind, it makes sense to use teams, task forces, and quality circles to allow employees to influence the important aspects of business decisions.

To conclude this discussion, it is important to mention that the old system of compensation based solely on traditional pay is no longer viable for the new era of globalization and the new economy. Most organizations today, are still using the old methods of compensation, but others are moving towards pay-for performance rewards. Under the new formula a base pay, linked to skills and competencies is used, the remainder of the compensation is linked to the organization's performance. This method provides organizations with more flexibility and links compensation to the ability to pay, thus possibly resulting in fewer layoffs in bad economic times.

We also looked at the effect of executive pay on both employee morale and shareholders' perceptions. It is apparent that in North America executive pay is becoming an issue, and it is time that some equity between employee and executive pay is brought into the discussion. A reform of current stock options agreement is also advocated prior to any introduction of such programs at other organizational levels. In order to create a reward system that benefits all concerned; that is executives, supervisory management and employees, it is important to involve all levels of staff in the design of the system.

Participative management works well when employees are used in the decision making process and the design and implementation of a new concept. Compensation and reward systems are no different. It must also be remembered that in today's high technology and fast world, money is not the only reward sought by employees. Organizations must factor in the non-monetary needs of the employee, flexibility in location and working hours, as well as the basics of recognition for a job well done, a simple thank you note, and most of all the fostering of self-respect and mutual support.

Tips for Success

REWARDS

Move away from job-based pay systems
Treat your employees as partners and pay them as owners
Pay for performance
Recognize employees' needs for extrinsic and intrinsic rewards
Money is not always the best reward
Increase holidays entitlement to increase productivity
Offer incentives, similar to top management, to rank-and-file workers
Balance fiscal responsibility with motivation of top performers

We must also remember that proper motivation backed by great rewards can produce continuous improvement in an organization. However, we must not forget that one of the greatest motivators in today's high paced and hi-tech environment is to . . .

CHAPTER 13

Use Your Employees' Creativity

"If you never change your mind, why have one?"
– Edward de Bono.

"The first and foremost rule of group creativity is to recognize that it is
a supplement and not a substitute for individual creativity."
– Michael LeBoeuf.

COMPETITION TODAY FORCES organizations to develop new and innovative ideas to keep up with the demands of the market place. To bring new products and services to the market organizations will be required to put in place a system that will tap into their employee's creativity to generate new ideas. As O'Reilly (1997) reported:

"Companies that know how to innovate don't necessarily throw money into R&D. Instead they cultivate a new style of corporate behavior that's comfortable with new ideas, change, risk, and even failure."

Collaboration is certainly a vehicle, which provides all employees with the opportunity to contribute to the decision-making process. In many organizations, especially hi-tech ones, teams and clusters are used to generate new ideas, and this method has proved to be very successful.

In the past decade many authors have discussed the use of creativity in the workplace, but few firms have taken heed and use it to their advantage. It is not that creativity did not exist in the workplace, but rather hierarchical structures and bureaucracy suppressed it. Competitiveness has suddenly brought the whole issue to the forefront of organizations' strategies and policies. Many firms today have special teams to discuss and formulate new strategies to make them more competitive. Courses on creativity are being held for employees to help them think creatively.

As a result a discussion on the issue of creativity in the workplace becomes significant. It is important to understand what creativity is, and how to tap the resources available to maximize its use in the workplace. There are a number of ways to involve employees in the decision-making process, and using their creativity is certainly an important element of the participative concept. I shall also discuss the reasons why creativity has been neglected and how employers have sometimes treated employees who show signs of being creative. In addition, I shall look at some techniques that can be used to increase the use of creativity and how it can be leveraged to benefit the organization. The objective is to examine and put forward a new strategy to maximize the use of one of the most underrated resources readily available in any organization – employees' creativity.

What is creativity?

The concept of creativity is associated with many human endeavors, including the arts, sciences, business and education. Creativity has made a comeback and we seem to be subjected to it constantly. Corporations and organizations train their employees to be more creative, education institutions stress that their students should be taught the process of being more creative. The number of books with titles using the word 'creative' is increasing geometrically. The concept of creativity is associated with many human endeavors, including the arts, sciences, business and education.

While we are bombarded by creativity in our daily life, we must first understand what it means before we can make full use of our mental powers in order to maximize our creative potential. The thought of producing a product or an idea, which is new and innovative, has been part of the human race for eons. In contrast, many new products have been the result of chance and accidents. For example Sir Alexander Fleming discovered penicillin because he left his Petri dish in the vicinity of a molding orange. Although it was an accident, Fleming had the ability to see a different pattern and make use of his findings. This is perhaps why

De Bono (1982) maintains that creativity is different from 'lateral thinking'. He states:

> "Lateral thinking is both an attitude of mind and also a number of defined methods. The attitude of mind involves the willingness to try to look at things in different ways. It involves an appreciation that any way of looking at things is only one amongst many possible ways. It involves an understanding of how the mind uses patterns and the need to escape from an established pattern to switch into a better one."[2]

People in all walks of life are creative at one time or another. Great chefs as well as great scientists are creative in their own ways. While their creation or invention may be different, the process used to achieve their goals is quite similar. In most cases they step out of their linear thinking pattern, and do something revolutionary and/or evolutionary to present us with something new. Creativity can then be defined, as: "the ability to generate new ideas or products which are unique and valuable".

I prefer the definition provided by John Kao (1996), who says:

> "I define creativity as the entire process by which ideas are generated, developed, and transformed into value. It encompasses what people commonly mean by innovation and entrepreneurship. In our lexicon, it connotes both the art of giving birth to new ideas and the discipline of shaping and developing those ideas to the stage of realized value."[3]

Now that we have established what creativity is, we should also discuss whether it is necessary to be intelligent to be creative. This discussion is very important because, if creativity were inherited like IQ, this would mean that it could not be learned or taught. Intelligence and creativity are related and fortunately for most of us recent evidence supports that creativity is really ability distinct from intelligence as defined by IQ tests. Sternberg[4] (1988).

While it has been shown that creativity and intelligence are related, it has further been put forward that motivation has an important role to play in creative work. In the context of participative management the aspect of motivation plays a major role in enhancing the creativity of employees. To engage employees in the decision-making process in order to tap into their creative abilities will also require that the proper motivation exists. This does not necessarily translate into financial rewards, but in most cases creativity is more closely related to intrinsic values. Organizations should understand that employees are not always receptive to purely material motivators, the satisfaction of being invited to be part of the process is sometime the best and only motivator required.

Motivation and Creativity

Most people are creative or can be taught to be creative, however the right conditions must exist in order to act as a catalyst. Motivation should be considered as one of the main catalyst in the creative process. Abraham Maslow (1943) argues that we have seven innate needs. They are as follows:

> Physiological Needs, Safety Needs, Love Needs, Esteem Needs, Self-Actualization Needs, Freedom of Inquiry, and Expression Needs, Knowledge and Understanding Needs
>
> In his opinion self-actualization ranks the highest on the hierarchy and he defines it this way: "A musician must make music, an artist must paint, a poet must write, if he is to be ultimately happy. What a man can be, he must be. This need we may call self-actualization . . . It refers to the desire for self-fulfillment, namely to the tendency for him to become actualized in what he is potentially . . . the desire to become more and more what one is, to become everything that one is capable of becoming."[5]

Although according to Maslow, very few of us reach that level of self-actualization, we all strive for it. One of the ways that organizations can help their employees towards this lofty goal is to provide them with the opportunity to be creative and achieve self-fulfillment. Through the establishment of a culture that promotes creativity organizations can provide employees with these intrinsic values, which can enhance their contribution to the organization as a whole.

Employees enjoy their work and want to contribute and do a good job. The role of the organization is to foster an atmosphere for them to perform at their highest level of achievement. Employees seek challenges and strive to solve problems if they are allowed to, otherwise their work can quickly become drab and boring, which usually result in low productivity and disenchantment. Given the right parameters and the opportunity to self-direct their actions, employees can very quickly embrace the concept of participative management, and increase their creativity. In today's ever increasing competitive business world, making use of all resources available has become a priority. Employee creativity is one enormous resource that many organizations have not or have been unwilling to use in the past. There are reasons for this lack of vision and misuse of employees' talents. Often it is the result of misconceptions and hierarchical organization structures.

Barriers to Creativity

Until very recently, few organizations believed in employees' participation in the decision-making process. This is changing. Hi-tech companies who have experienced tremendous success and growth by using self-directed and cross-functional teams to solve difficult problems and produce innovative ideas have showed the way. Why this trend for teams and participative management took so long to emerge is deeply rooted in organizational culture. Most organizations believe in a well-defined hierarchy with levels of supervision and control. This culture usually promotes segregation rather than collaboration.

Promotion is based on the ability to conform, control and supervise, rather than knowledge. The decision-making process in these organizations is top-down, with very little input by lower level employees. These organizations also believe that people at the top have all the answers, because they usually are more knowledgeable, experienced and have earned their place in the hierarchy. However, as stated earlier, intelligence does not necessarily equate to creativity. In fact intelligent people are often rigid in their thinking and possess enormous egos that often prevent them from being creative.

The constraints of intelligence and conformity may play a greater role than we think in blocking creativity. This is perhaps why young children are more creative when they play. As De Bono (1976) states:

> "Up to the age of ten or eleven a child's ego is separable from his thinking. He enjoys thinking. He enjoys playing with ideas. he is wrong so often that his security is not dependent on his being right. After the age of eleven thinking becomes very much part of his ego and self-image. A person is as good as his thinking."

We know that in hierarchical and bureaucratic organizations, there is very little room for free thinking. Everything is governed by rules and procedures, which leaves very little left to imagination or creativity. The need for conforming in order to rise to the top is a major constraint to creative thinking. Risk and making mistakes are not tolerated in this environment; it is more likely that the assignment of blame takes precedence over problem solving. In fact in many organizations, creative people are regarded as mavericks and are branded as disturbers and non-team members. These barriers must be removed to allow for the free flow of information and the exchange of ideas from all levels of the workforce. This is one reason why organizations, which transformed themselves from pyramidal to flatter structures, are benefiting from the participation of their employees in the decision-making process. Organizations, which use the creative participation of their employees, are leveraging themselves against the competition. Those who do not will most likely fail and face the fate of the Dodo.

Fostering Creativity

Earlier we said that creativity must not only be encouraged but there must be some motivation to make it work. Organizations, which use their employees' creativity to solve problems and become innovative, have developed a culture that fosters creativity. These organizations have used the change process to promote self-directed teams and train their employees into thinking creatively. They have built the right climate for the creative process to blossom. They allow for mistakes and do not punish risk taking. As a result, their employees approach problems by getting out of the 'pigeon holes', which exist, in most bureaucratic organizations. Creative thinking in these new organizations does not require courage and is certainly not accompanied by the fear of failure.

When the climate is right for creativity, it is also right for motivating employees. Many organizations reward their employees for creative ideas by means of material rewards. Material rewards are great, but in many cases the achievement of success and the recognition of their efforts are often enough to motivate employees for their creativity and contribution to the organization's bottom line. Edward Glassman (1991) states:

> "If you want creativity, make sure the rewards for creative efforts are equal to, or exceed, those for good performance on approved projects. Emphasize the submission of new ideas in job descriptions and performance reviews and in the reward process. And give the creative person the assistance he or she needs to develop the idea for the team review, and implement it if that's what the person wants to do." [6]

It is important to recognize employees' contributions and their creative collaboration in the decision making process, but it is also important to provide them with the tools to be creative.

How to be Creative?

The tools provided to improve creativity at work may be state-of-the-art creativity procedures, the proper climate or out-of-the-box procedures, but most importantly the proper training must be provided. The objectives of a training program for creativity should include, among other things, freeing participants from their perceptions, their fear of failure and injecting fun into the work environment. Let us look at some of the ideas that can help people become more creative in the workplace.

Dealing with Perceptions

Very often the inability to be creative can be traced to our perceptions, or the way we look at things. One of the problems we have is that we often associate perception with knowledge. In fact this is not true, perception is the way we view available knowledge, and how we direct our attention over available knowledge. One of the common misconceptions is that not all people are creative, and this can often lead us to forget to be creative. If we have a belief that we are not creative, more likely that not, we are not going to use our thinking powers to be creative. It is therefore, important to remember and be reminded to be creative.

To be creative we must keep our minds open to new suggestions. Perceptions can stop us from being objective in our thinking. Tunnel vision is usually the result of egocentricity. In order to be creative, we must remember that the world does not revolve around us. Arrogance and conceit follow very closely and distorts our perception of things. In a team environment there is no room for participants to be arrogant, egocentric or conceited. To maximize the use of creativity these traits and misconceptions must be left at the door. For example, the perception that an engineer is better qualified than a mechanic to express his opinion about the building of a bridge is totally out of place in a creative context. Everyone on the team is an equal partner and has something valuable to offer. In cross-functional, as well as multi-discipline teams, no one is more or less qualified. In fact sometimes what seems to be stupid or insignificant can very often trigger the switch that produces the creative solution.

What is important in being creative is to gather accurate information, and use it properly. As stated by John Kao(1996):

> "Creativity begins with the *generation* of ideas. It is also very much at work in the selection, development, and implementation of ideas. When people brainstorm, some members of the group may simply spew derivative, top-of-mind stuff. There's no "get" to it, no reaching out. Often though, by acknowledging the creativity of selection and implementation, the more generative participants in the group will recognize and acknowledge the off-the-shelf quality of their thinking and will reach into new "territories" for something fresher and stronger."[7]

The more information is available, the better the solution is likely to be. With good information it is less likely that solutions will be based on partialism. While partialism – a form of bias, which is based on inadequacy of perception, can be intentional or unintentional; in both cases the result will be incorrect. Whether partialism was intentional or not, if the decision is based on inadequate information then the mistake will never be detected.

Getting rid of our perceptions and promote the creative process can be helped by means of a few procedures. While linear thinking is an acceptable way of getting new and useful ideas, non-linear thinking can be used to jump-start a process, which is getting nowhere. Thinking in a multitude of context, can often free us from the rut we are in and sometimes even the introduction of the bizarre and the unusual can be beneficial.

If and when a process is slowing down, making a problem more visual can help the creative process. Make use of models and sketches to help remove the barrier to creativity. Because more space in our brain is devoted to visualizing things, often a visual representation can help remove the perception, which prevents us from solving the problem. In fact it is suggested that taking notes during creative meetings should be done by means of mind maps. The use of color, images, shapes, dimensions, words, symbols, lines and circles tend to satisfy the needs of the whole brain, and stimulate creativity, as well as remove obstacles.

Removing the Fear of Failure

One of the greatest obstacles to creativity is the fear of failure. Some organizations have instilled the fear of failure in their employees, through management by 'stick and carrot'. In participative management that fosters creative thinking, there are ways to remove that fear, and allow employees' contributions to flourish.

First employees should be encouraged to keep trying to do their best in spite of the possibility of failure. It is important that the right behavior exists amongst participants. In western society, many of our problem-solving decisions are made in an adversarial context. When a positive creative climate is absent it is necessary to shape the behavior of participants to be more receptive to other members' ideas and show courage in deferring ideas which may not be useful. The word 'no' should be banished when confronted with new ideas, because negative feelings cannot be part of the creative process. If you believe that you cannot do something, you won't do it. It is that simple. In order to keep creative levels high, any dispute or disagreement should be negotiated immediately. Advocating three responses to ideas can surmount negativism. The **PIN** method can be used effectively to get back on track. The **PIN** method forces the group to focus on the **Positive**, and **Interesting** aspect of the problem in order to banish the **Negative**, it can refocus the group before they reach an initial judgment.

Of course to get people working together, it always helps to have well-organized meetings. Creativity meetings are no less different, and we suggest that the following plan be adopted to gain maximum benefit from your meetings. In addition, well-planned meetings remove uncertainty, and the possibility of any in fighting because the agenda sets the path for the meeting.

In trying to solve a problem creatively, a well-designed system should be used. A set of steps or sequence should be adopted to help focus on the issue and the task at end. The following is a general guideline:

1st Step: Define the problem in detail; provide a list of problem statements to help the group think in different context.

2nd Step: Select the reason, or criteria for the final outcome

3rd Step: Choose reasonable statements, which best define the problem

4th Step: Use Brainstorming, or a similar exercise, to produce as many ideas as possible

5th Step: Identify criteria (feasibility, constraints, cause and effect, benefits, etc.,) to select ideas.

6th Step: Mix all ideas to generate creative proposals to achieve new and useful solutions.

If this format seems to be too stringent, it is so to provide structure. Although we have said that creativity sometimes comes out of chaos, the suggested format helps to focus and keep out unwanted distractions. It also helps to focus on the intrinsic values, of self-motivation and enjoyment. We should also try to resist the promise of extrinsic rewards while focusing on creativity. The immediate self-actualization reward is more conducive to creativity, and the other rewards will follow automatically.

Discipline and isolation to help concentration and focus, does not mean that fun should be excluded from the process. On the contrary, humor, as a means to stimulate the creative juices is strongly advocated.

Humor and Creativity

It is said that those who play together work well together. If this is true, it is amazing to see that most organizations do not foster a playful atmosphere for their employees. In large bureaucratic organizations, there are rules for everything, from a dress code to the use of music in the workplace. The potential of humor and frivolity in the workplace has been greatly ignored in the past, and it is time that the rigidity and conformity be replaced by some fun. This is not a passing comment on the current work environment, but research supports the fact that humor should be used to increase creativity in the workplace. De Bono (1982) remarked:

> "It has amazed me how little attention philosophers, psychologists and information theorists have paid to humour. Humour is probably the most significant characteristic of the human mind. It tells us much more about how the system works than does anything else."

More people and organizations are finally accepting that a playful approach to problem solving may guarantee better results. Humor has certain characteristics that cannot be found anywhere else. It is a combination of sensations, which brings happiness and enjoyment, while being anti-arrogant, and fosters humility and tolerance. Humor creates a positive atmosphere, which can be mind opening. If you listen to someone else's story, she or he is ready to listen to yours. This opens the door for an exchange of ideas and more open communication.

Humor also opens the mind to enable the vision of things to come in different ways. Child's play often is very creative and can be used to break the ice in a team environment. For example take this question from a child's game: 'what is yellow and white and travels at 500 miles an hour? – The answer is a Boeing 747 pilot's egg sandwich'.

A playful approach to problem solving is gradually finding its place in the work environment. The use of humor, as well as child like play to solve problems is fast becoming part of organization's strategies. Novation and critical thinking are being practiced in organizations such as Chrysler and NASA. These techniques are used to rejuvenate employees. Simple brainstorming techniques and power thinking stimulated with the use of toys and artifacts are used to increase employee creativity. Toys such as Play-Doh and silly putty are increasingly used to put employees into a playful state of mind. The rigidity of organizations and their obsession with action has, in many cases, produced a disconnection between action and the thought process, resulting in management fads such as re-engineering and downsizing. It is important to bring back some of the fun in the working place by letting employees acts like children from time to time. Humor also brings with it a certain humility, which no longer exists, in certain bureaucratic organizations. Ken Blanchard (1997) says it best:

> "Humility and humor go hand in hand. An attitude of humility is an ingredient of successful change because it permits people to take what they do seriously, while at the same time taking themselves lightly. People with humility don't think less of themselves – they just think about themselves less. Because they're willing to admit their own limitations, they tend to be willing team players."

Summary

While organizations are asking their employees to do more with less, many employees feel that they can do more to help their organizations, but their abilities are not being utilized. Collaborative management can provide a vehicle for organizations to tap into this vast amount of creativity left unused amongst their workforce. What is required is a change in culture and the fostering of creativity for the sake of achieving excellence by both the organization and the employee.

A new culture, which promotes creativity, must embrace the recognition of contributors, not necessarily through extrinsic but through intrinsic rewards.

Tips for Success

ENHANCE CREATIVITY

Hire creative people
Let them be creative
Identify the boundaries of the 'BOX'
Get out of the 'BOX'
The crazier the ideas the better
Create a culture of 'Fun and Humour'
Get out of the way

CHAPTER 14

Support

"If corporate entrepreneurs have to be skilled at building coalitions, it is equally true that the company environment in which they operate has to help them clear the way."

– Rosabeth Moss Kanter.

A S ORGANIZATIONS RESTRUCTURE themselves to become more competitive, often this is done through downsizing and flattening of the organization's structure. When this occurs it is meaningful to recognize the effects of these drastic, sometimes radical, changes and the impact on trust within the organization. In this context support is used to cover a wide range of issues, most of them pertaining to the welfare of employees, whether they are still employed or leaving the organization as a result of restructuring.

Employees who stay need nurturing and require their trust in the organization reinforced. For those unfortunate employees who have been let go, a different approach is required. In addition, it is important that organizations start to support not only their employees, but they should start looking at their roles within the larger community, and seek means to support that community in certain projects.

We can see that the issue of corporate support extends its boundaries far beyond the immediate employee. To this effect, we must look at the responsibilities of the business organization beyond the larger context of profit making. While it is important for organizations to look after the bottom line, it is also incumbent upon them to maintain a certain responsibility to the community, which ultimately supports them. To the extent that support is closely linked to both the immediate employees and the community at large, we shall examine this issue both as an internal and an external matter. The internal context will look at all the desired support needed in today's organizations to create harmony between employees' needs and those of organizations. The external context will include the supporting role of organizations *vis-a-vis* the community at large.

Internal Support

Organizations do have a responsibility for their employees. While good management involves the constant search for ways to support employees, managers must be involved in monitoring the quality and frequency of support given to individuals and teams. As mentioned before, it is not only current employees who require support but also those employees who have been displaced through restructuring. While the immediate concern of the organization should be reserved for its current workforce it must not neglect its former employees when it has been decided to part company. The whole idea of support is to make employees comfortable and remove anxiety. When an atmosphere of trust exists, it is easier to gain employees' confidence, which eventually results in productivity and collaboration. Let us look at the many facets of employee support.

Health and Safety

An organization concerned with its employees' safety and welfare will spend quite a lot of money on these issues, and they are also usually rewarded in many ways. By providing a safe and healthy working environment, organizations can increase their productivity by decreasing the number of staff-days lost due to accidents or illness. When employees feel safer in a healthy environment the organization will save on insurance premiums and other costs associated with lost working days. To the credit of many organizations, safety committees were formed to look into the safety and health of manual workers, who were most likely to be exposed to health and safety hazards. This issue is no longer restricted to factory or manual workers, but now increasingly include office staff.

Technology adds another form of stress. To keep pay cheques coming in employees have to adapt to electronic gadgets that increasingly become part of the everyday work environment. Many employees take to these gadgets like duck to water, however many others find it very stressful. A recent survey undertaken in 13 countries by Priority Management, an international consulting company revealed that 80% of workers felt stress regularly, while 25% felt stress everyday. While technology has often made life easier, it also is a cause of stress because it blurs the boundaries between work time and leisure time. Let us look at some facts about stress in the work place:

- 30% of adults say that stress impacts life
- The United States spends $800 million on stress medication per year.
- Job stress is very often caused by high demands and the lack of control.
- Many employees need the right challenge and stress level to perform better

With the proliferation of computers in the work environment a number of safety issues have arisen in the office environment. The high incidence of repetitive strain related injuries, such as carpal tunnel syndrome, and eyesight problems due to long hours in front of computer terminals needs to be addressed by companies for the safety and health of their employees. To combat this increasing stress inhibitor, workers must set priorities and set time aside for proper exercise, relaxation and proper eating.

The support of organizations requires the provision of better-lit environment and workstations, which are more ergonomically designed to help employees minimize the effect of the new workplace disease. It is also wise to allow employees to take frequent breaks in order to perform certain exercises that will keep them healthy and productive. Too many long and extended periods in front of a computer has proven to be unhealthy and cause what could be long-term problems for employees. Organizations should look into all aspects of the work environment to minimize the health and safety risk to which their employees may be subjected.

It should be remembered that a healthy employee is more likely to be more productive. Fortunately industry leaders are addressing many of these issues. For example at SAS Institute, a software developer company, employees get free massage, 35 hours/week with flexible schedules, ergonomic work environment, and on site medical and health care. In addition, they have a company-subsidized cafeteria with a piano player for lunch, and a 'putting green' close to a fully equipped gymnasium.

Counseling

The physical well being of employees should not be the only concern of an organization. The pressures resulting from change may have some serious impact on the health of employees. Change is very stressful and organizations should ensure that there are programs in place to deal with these situations. Counseling, either in house or outsourced, should be made available. Often just a short talk with a counselor can alleviate many of the anxieties, which employees develop as a result of pressures brought about by change. Employees need reassurance and reinforcement that they are wanted and are part of the organization. The need for psychological support is more important after a downsizing strategy, because the surviving employees are often put under more stress, due to increase workload or responsibility. Many employees can cope with the change, but often some employees may have great difficulty in adapting to the new environment. The organization as the instigator of change should also be responsible for the support of the surviving employees.

In addition we are seeing many problems related to social change that also have an impact upon the state of employees health. Alcoholism and drug addiction are problems, which are becoming part of a difficult social fabric. Employees should be helped and encouraged to seek help to alleviate these problems. Many organizations have drug and addiction policies in place, however dismissal should not always be the preferred action. Many employees afflicted by these social ills, may have fallen prey as a result of work related stress. What are required are understanding, treatment and rehabilitation. On the job drug or alcohol addiction must be recognized and dealt with as soon as possible. Intoxicated workers are more prone to accidents and injuries; on top of that, they may become a safety hazard to their fellow workers. Under all these circumstances the organization has an important role to play.

Employees affected by any one of these problems deserve the support of their employers; they should not be discarded and left to society to care for. Very often it is the stress to which they may be subjected to at work that causes these problems in the first place. Although employees must take responsibility for their actions, direct or indirect corporate support should be made available to help them get out of their inflicted plight.

Mentoring

While psychological and counseling support is advocated for people with addiction or stress related problems, other employees also require a support system. The development of a good workforce, more specifically for those employees who have displayed the potential for higher levels of performance is crucial to the continuing growth of an organization. In this case the type of support we refer to is mentoring.

Many organizations encourage internal or external mentoring. The process is very simple, because it is the matching of an employee with a more senior person who would serve as a guide for the development of the chosen employee. It requires dedication from both mentor and protégé, and commitment is the key to the success of this process. The more experienced partner in this relationship serves as a guide, and counselor to the junior partner. Experiences pertaining to the job are passed and the formation of the protégé is undertaken. Mentoring provides even managers with rudimentary people skills – a method to support and develop their subordinates.

However much I agree with mentoring, I have a word of caution. While mentoring is a desired process for developing chosen potential successors for an organization, sometimes it can result into problems. In many cases the existing corporate culture may be passed along to the new generation, and if there is no will to improve the culture, this process may result in cloning. It is hoped that a mentorship program involves the appropriate selection and matching of the mentor and the protégé. The selection should take into account future strategies and objectives of the organization.

While the process can become a rewarding experience it can also have severe impact on the future of the organization. Another problem with mentoring is especially evident in 'abusive' corporations. When a mentor leaves the organization, either voluntarily or involuntarily downsized, the protégé may very quickly become a victim of the organization, because of his/her association with the mentor.

The adoption of a mentorship program provides the participants with a feeling of satisfaction. The protégé receives the knowledge and support required for his or her development. Mentors become teachers, motivated by love for their work, and through the respect for others in the organization they do everything to pass on the torch, which will far outlive their achievements. This is an unselfish attitude worth including in any corporate culture. Mentorship is a support given to others by true leaders who are interested in the well being of others and the success of an organization. These leaders recognize that they may disappear, but their ideas and principles would have been passed to a new generation for the future.

Team Support

In the new environment where teams are increasingly used to either solve problems or just work together on projects, support becomes very important. While we talked about a support system involving a superior and a subordinate, it is equally important that team members learn to support each other. The success of any team depends on harmony. Real team members should support a process that allows every member the opportunity to express his or her opinion. The culture of the team should be based on mutual support for ideas, proposals, and decisions. Team members who may not agree entirely with the outcome of a discussion should under the process of consensus support the team's decision.

In the collaborative environment the idea is that people who participate in the decision-making process are more likely to actively contribute in the implementation. However, for the implementation to be a success consensus is required. If management creates a culture that supports the decision made by teams, it is more likely that team members will support each other during and after working together.

As Beck & Hillmar(1986) said:

> "To accomplish teamwork, managers must be aware of their own as well as team members' needs for interpersonal skills. They must let the members know how they wish them to operate with each other in support and accountability."

This type of culture will help to fortify the bonds between team members and between employees and the organization. It can be achieved through leadership by example, and/or through appropriate training.

Training and Development

As we mentioned earlier, training and development has become a major concern for employee and employers alike. Employers need better-educated staff to keep up with the technological revolution and to increase productivity in a competitive world. Organizations require training for their staff to work as a team or to develop individual skills. The introduction of cross functions into companies for the optimization of performance makes it important to train people. Training does not stop at staff level, but must also include executives. In fact Dan Dimancescu (1992) said:

> "Senior executives or managers who institute a program must **train themselves** in cross function process methods before they delegate a follow-up. They must be committed for the long haul."[2]

Employees on the other hand, want training to maintain and develop their skills for two main reasons. One to keep up with developments, which affect their current position, and two, continually improve themselves to be employable in a fast changing employment market. Since job security is a thing of the past, employees want their companies to train them in new skills that will help them add value wherever they are.

The role of organizations is to provide and/or facilitate training opportunities for its workforce. The support may be financial, whereby employees are either reimbursed for upgrading their skills, as long as they benefit the company, or they may be given paid time off to attend extracurricular courses. In-house training provided for by company staff or outside consultants, should be planned to give employees the opportunity to learn new skills pertaining to their jobs, and also the opportunity to interact with other employees outside of the strict working environment.

Mavericks in the Organization

When we talk about support, we tend to look at the issue as it concerns people we like or those who fit the system. In many cases it is important to sit back and look at those employees who do not quite fit the mold of the average employee. Some organizations do support this type of employee and through their contribution gain either competitive advantage or new territory. Xerox Corp., for example, supported Pavel Curtis to create a 'virtual community' on the Internet, called 'The Land of MOO'.

These workers are the ones, usually referred to as misfits, mavericks and disgruntled, because very often these employees do not seem to fit the norm and often operate from what seems to be a different set of references Nelson, Good and Hill (1997) provide a description of mavericks, they state:

> "Mavericks have a unique picture of reality. Anything is negotiable, and the higher the stakes, the better. Because they value freedom more than possessions or relationships, they are likely to be easily frustrated by people who avoid risks. While they may not believe it is their job to change the views of others, they do want those who confine them to get out of the way and let them do what they need to do."[3]

With those given characteristics, mavericks are the people to call upon to respond to crises. Mavericks in management are praised for their boldness and their achievements, Jaclyn Fierman (1995) reported:

> "Unconventional leaders share an ability to stun the competition with their personal brand of can-doism. At a time when all leads are only temporary, they're exactly what's called for."[4]

The *Fortune* article goes on to praise such 90s successes including Ricardo Semler of Semco – Brazil, Doug Nelson of Philip Morris – USA, and Richard Branson of Virgin – UK. Unfortunately, in recent years many maverick employees have been the victims of management decisions while undergoing an organization restructuring. In fact research has shown that many of them have been 'abused' and 'victimized'. Wright and Smye (1996) wrote:

> "Some corporations keep staggering along, disguising the lack of ideas with high turnover. They keep taking new people on board, swiping their fresh ideas, slowly silencing them with abusive culture, then firing them and starting all over."[5]

The 'Downsized'

When a corporation restructures and in so doing has to resort to a reduction in staff, those who are downsized should not be forgotten. These employees, through no fault of their own, are let go by the corporation and they should be given support to cope with this very traumatic situation. The corporation should provide counseling, financial and in many cases some psychological support.

Too often companies in recent years have treated their employees like 'dirt'. In some cases, employees have been escorted to the parking lot by security guards after they have been given notice of their termination. Financial packages have been used to pay off and get rid of employees with the bare minimum as prescribed by industrial and labor laws. Many of these employees find themselves in difficult financial situations, and those who are in their fifties find it extremely hard to get a new job. While corporations are supposedly cutting costs, the downsizing movement has actually put a heavy burden on government programs due to the increasing number of unemployed.

Many companies get rid of their employees in a very insensitive way. However, it must be mentioned that other corporations have gone through the same process with more humanity and consideration for their employees. While financial packages have been somewhat lucrative in some cases, there have been other things that companies have done for their former employees. At Nova Corporation of Calgary, for instance, downsized employees received in addition to a financial package, counseling and financial help to open new businesses. This type of support helped many employees find new careers or new jobs. Their entrepreneurial skills were recognized and they are contributing to society. They have not become a burden to society and in many cases have found happiness and success in their new endeavors. Many of these former employees were awarded outsourcing contracts by Nova to kick-start their new business.

Corporations must not discard their employees like dirty linen. They should not forget that these same employees are members of a larger community and are, or can be their future customers. The other side of the coin is that any massive lay off can affect the economy of the community, hence can affect the company. Corporations have a duty to the community in which they operate, and the well being of their current and former employees are their responsibility.

External Support

Since corporations have a role to play within the community, their support should extend to programs within the community where they operate. As a good citizen corporations should provide support for activities and the general development of the community at large. In many cases, the private and the public sector are forming alliances to provide programs in the community. The arts and culture have, for a very long time, benefited from the support of corporations. Nowadays we can see corporate support being extended to include education, healthcare and charities. Two examples of philanthropic corporate deeds come to mind. The first one being the donation of hundreds of millions of dollars by Microsoft's Bill Gates and his wife to fund a program of child vaccination in the third world. The second one is the commitment of Morris Chang's company TSMC of Taiwan to fund a foundation for the benefit of education, the arts and the community at large.

As funding from governments decreases, corporations must take up the slack. In many instances corporations have allowed some of their senior employees to work for charities, such as the United Way. These executives provide some valuable expertise to these not-for-profit organizations. In return the company gets better skilled workers who are more understanding of the problems outside of the corporation. The employee gains a 'psychic reward' from the experience and often comes back to the corporation refreshed and reinvigorated.

In hard economic times however, the best way for a corporation to show community support is to evaluate carefully the impact of closure and downsizing on the immediate community. Very often corporations make decisions based on the 'bottom line' and 'short-term profits'; notwithstanding the disastrous effect that their decisions may have on their former employees and the community at large. However, there are some organizations that take their community responsibility very seriously. This can be illustrated by the story of Malden Mills.

In 1995 Malden Mills a textile company in Lawrence Massachusetts, was burnt to the ground. In these days where textiles are produced at a cheaper rate in third world countries, it would have been easy for management to pack up and set up shop in South East Asia. For Aaron Feuerstein the President of Malden Mills it was a different decision. It was decided that the factories would be rebuilt and that all full time employees would be kept on the payroll. The reported costs to the company were approximately $10 million. In March of 1996, most of workforce is back to work in new factories producing their well-known product 'Polartec' a synthetic fleece used in the production of outerwear. The commitment of Feuerstein to the community and to his employees is reflected in the early results, as reported by Shelley Donald Coolidge (1996):

> "The investment has already begun to pay off: the quality and efficiency of production are better today than before the fire, Feuerstein says. For example, in one of the Polartec finishing plans that wasn't destroyed, the plant produced about 130,000 yards of the fabric a week prior to the fire, Today, production is double that.

In addition, before the fire, 6 to 7 percent of what was manufactured was off-quality, he says. Now, that number has dropped to 2 percent. "this is a direct result of the goodwill and determination of our people to show their gratitude to Malden Mills," he notes." [6]

But the most incredible part of this story is that it was the second time in the 90 years history of the company that Feuerstein has saved the community. In 1980 Malden Mills declared bankruptcy, but recovered and hired back every laid-off worker. These rare corporate actions saved a community from economic disaster and gained a committed workforce through trust and support. In addition to increased productivity in 1996, it is also reported that Malden Mills, benefited from approximately $50 million of free advertising through newspaper and television reports on the story of the company and of its philanthropic President Aaron Feuerstein.

Corporate support is important, whether it be for its immediate employees, past employees or the community. Employees who feel trusted are more likely to contribute to the success of the organization. While it is important to create a culture of support for current employees and the teams within an organization, it also meaningful to remember those employees who are laid-off in hard economic times. Downsized employees who are properly supported by their former organizations are more likely to contribute to the economy and the society at large. Those who are discarded summarily may become a burden on society and also cause the company harm in the future. Corporate support for the immediate community can extend from financial help to employees participation in civic and community affairs. In return, very often the financial results of a corporation can be attributed to its commitment and support for its employees and the community.

In the past chapters we have examined the different principles involved in inspiring and maintaining trust. The adoption and practice of these principles would be wasted in a collaborative environment if management did not make a serious effort to include all parties concerned in making . . .

CHAPTER 15

Team Decisions

"Me, We."

– Muhammad Ali.

"The essence of a team is common commitment."

– Jon Katzenbach.

M OST, IF NOT all of the concepts and ideas we have shared so far in this book would not be appropriate if team decisions were not an integral part of the process. In a participative environment that fosters collaboration, interaction and the sharing of ideas it would be remiss if in the final decision making process the individuals involved did not have a say. Team decision is the last of the five principles put forward for the attainment and maintenance of trust in organizations.

Increasingly organizations are finding that the use of teams can be more responsive to the challenges of a more competitive world. The complexities of the job and information overload have made it more difficult for managers to make all the decisions. One of the fallacies of current human resource strategies, is that employees should be managed.

Management implies control and the exertion of power. Fortunately, it is being realized that the people who are closest to the problem, since they have more information best make decisions. The old autocratic and coercive pyramidal hierarchies, with their authoritative management style did not result in productive and loyal employees. They are fortunately being replaced with flatter organizations, which make better use of teamwork and consensus in their decision making process.

A team is defined by Martin & Hackett (1993) as:

> "A collection of people (usually 5-9) who rely on cooperation, trust and communication in order to achieve their goals and objectives."

In a team, individuals have their own ideas to share with the group. It is important that a proper facilitation process exists to promote harmony and allow contribution. All members of the team must be allowed the opportunity to express his or her opinion without fear of repercussions or ridicule. Good facilitation and harmony is the result of proper planning and organization of meetings. In the spirit of collaboration we shall also discuss the decision-making process with an emphasis on conflict management and reaching consensus.

Team v/s Individuals

In western society we have been accustomed to individualism. Most of our achievements and accomplishment measurements are geared to the success of the individual. We are more comfortable in acknowledging the success of one individual as opposed to a group, or team of individuals. Until more recently this cult of the individual was the norm with the exception of sports where teams are more regularly recognized for their successes. The overwhelming success of Japanese companies changed the concept of individualism. In fact the world has become fascinated with bottom-up and consensus decision-making process, which is the corner stone of successful Japanese organizations. As a result, more western organizations are gradually moving towards teamwork as a preferred organizational structure.

The basic nature of team decision is to be able to manage conflict and reach consensus. Team decisions reached, preferably by involving all stakeholders in the problem-solving process, results in two main advantages: additional brainpower to find a solution, and increased support during the implementation stage. This has been demonstrated in high technology companies, which have used teams for the development of software and other computer applications with great success. Now this concept is increasingly being used in all types of industries and organizations.

In the past, ideas came from the top and workers had to implement them without much contribution in the decision making process. The teamwork concept has been very slow to catch on in most western companies, because the organizational structure was so pyramidal. The structures were always dominated by one person at the very top, followed by a few managers, or layers of supervisors with the majority of the workers at the bottom of the pyramid. As we move towards a more participative management style, we are finding that no individual, no matter how qualified or skilled, can provide a better solution than a team. Although individual members of a team have different ideas, perceptions and behavior, the results of working together have proved that the synergism of a group's mental ability, information and skills have always been better than the efforts of an individual. Anyone, no matter how skilled, can learn or be stimulated by the ideas of others who may be less knowledgeable.

However, by advocating the concept of team decision making, I do not suggest removing leaders, or individual thinkers and decision makers from the process. Instead, I suggest that if organizations want participation and partnership, everyone in the organization should be given the opportunity to contribute towards achieving that goal. Leaders in this new environment will no longer be the controllers of old, but will rather become the facilitators of tomorrow. Their new role will be to enable the process of team decision-making by running effective meetings and blend individual and collective wisdom. Daniel Tagliere (1992) said:

> "Great leaders are those who pursue new visions, encourage individual initiative, and value and know how to, meet, think, and work participatively with the best minds available."[2]

It is not that leaders will disappear in this new environment. Instead their contributions will be more geared to the success of the organization and its group of employees, rather than towards individual accomplishment. They will require new skills and competencies more specifically associated with reaching consensus and conflict resolution.

Conflict Management and Resolution

Conflict is a fact of life. Although it may not be a daily occurrence, it is bound to affect us more often than not. It is therefore important for us to learn how to resolve rather than try to avoid it. Conflict in the work environment used to be viewed as negative and destructive, usually associated with employees viewed as difficult and non-cooperative. Fortunately, today, behavioral experts have told us that it is a natural occurrence and that in fact if managed properly it can have very positive results. As more people work together to solve problems, it becomes important for us to recognize that conflict does exist and that we should learn to deal with it, rather than ignore it.

The success of an organization will depend largely on the ability to manage conflict. Today's work environment has made the management of conflict an important skill that should be highly developed to cope with the effects of change. Added pressures will come to bear as globalization and increasing number of employees from different ethnic and cultural backgrounds enter the workforce. As more organizations move towards structures based on teams, we understand that conflict will occur and this environment will require effective leaders and team members who understand the value of conflict resolution and management.

Sources of Conflict

Conflict in the workplace is usually of two major types, interpersonal and organizational. The former is more prevalent because it based on individual beliefs and values, which determines behavior. It usually occurs because an individual or group perceives a situation or problem in a different way from others. Our core beliefs are determined and imprinted in the early stages of our childhood and adolescence, while our values are determined by significant events in our adulthood. Occasionally these beliefs and values are challenged in the workplace and can become the source of interpersonal conflicts. While we cannot change the core beliefs and values, we can learn new ways to help modify our behavior. In so doing we can open our personal horizons, promote personal development and at the same time start looking at other people under different lights.

Organizational conflict, on the other hand, is not based on individual values and beliefs but it is rather a result of changing dynamics within a structure. Although change occurs within organizations, the usual ones such as procedures, policies and relocation do not cause too much conflict. On the other hand layoffs, downsizing or demassing, may create upheavals in the work environment. Conflicting goals and objectives between departments, as well as, the lack of resources to attain and maintain expected performance can also be a source of organizational conflict. If not managed properly, these conflicts can result in interpersonal conflicts. In many cases organizational conflict is the result of bad communication, and it is incumbent upon management to ensure the minimization of its effects upon employees in order to prevent additional interpersonal conflicts.

While we cannot always resolve it, nor should we avoid it, we can manage conflict to some form of conclusion. In western societies, especially North American, where the adversarial culture is more prevalent, we seem to have more conflict. Everyone seems to be in competition with each other, and there seems to be an attempt at complete dominance or even winning at all costs. In order to manage conflict we should examine the five commonly used methods

Methods for Resolving Conflict

The following is a description of the five methods commonly used to resolve conflict. They are different and each one should be used under the appropriate circumstances to reach a desired conclusion to a conflict.

Win/Lose

The win/lose resolution is focused on 'winning at all cost'. It has its roots in competition, and is an attempt to dominate the situation completely without any search for an appropriate solution for everyone involved. All sources of power available are put to use to resolve the conflict. Position power through rank or superiority, economic power and sometimes, even force will be used to reach a conclusion. The characteristics of this methodology, may lead to the belief that it cannot be used successfully in the workplace, but there are circumstances when it may be appropriate. They are:

- When a quick decision is required – in a crisis
- When unpopular changes have to be implemented
- In bureaucratic, and autocratic organizations, or where low trust exists
- When there are no other alternatives

Lose/Win

In contrast to competition, the accommodation method results in a lose/win situation. In this method there is an assertive choice to be non-assertive. It is used when there is a willingness to yield to the other party's position. Assertive accommodation is not avoidance of a conflict. This method can be used when:

- The value of the relationship is more important than the issue
- The issue is less important to you than it is to the other party
- You want to show a degree of reasonableness
- It is important to encourage others to express their opinions

Lose/Lose

Non-assertive avoidance of a conflict may give the impression that there is an unwillingness to cooperate, denial of the existence of a problem, or even backing-off from the issue. In this case, there is a forfeiture of personal gain and the reluctance to work towards a reasonable solution. In the lose/lose situation, there is no management of conflict, let alone resolution, because neither party is able to deal with the problem. This method can be used effectively when:

- There is an impasse, and nothing is getting anywhere
- A temporary 'time out' or 'cooling off' period is appropriate
- The issue can be effectively resolve by others
- The negative impact of continuing can be too damaging to both parties

Win/Lose – Win/Lose

This approach to conflict resolution, better known as the compromise, involves negotiation, exchange, swapping, tradeoffs and most of all, flexibility. The use of this method implies that each party will gain some, but will also have to give some to reach resolution. In this case, it is therefore wise to know in advance how much one is willing to give away. While you may not have to give away everything, setting limits before the negotiation starts provides a benchmark or objective for effective negotiation. The compromise method is an attempt to find common ground of agreement while showing a concern for ones objectives, as well as the importance of the relationship. It can be used when:

- Important objectives can be preserved, while maintaining the relationship
- There is willingness to go to the root of the problem
- Both parties are willing to accept, and understand each other's feelings
- The parties are willing to explore together alternatives, which may not have been thought of individually.

The techniques mentioned above are best used to resolve conflict of an interpersonal nature. Let us now, look at some additional steps that can be used to resolve organizational conflict.

Peer Reviews

Unlike the peer review mentioned in conjunction with appraisals (see Chapter 10), a similar panel can be used to settle employee-employer disputes. This concept should not be restricted to unionized employees, but should be made available to middle and senior management as well. To be successful such a program must be properly initiated.

A peer review system requires that the company trains a pool of volunteer employees who will serve as a jury of their fellow workers. The individual members undertake a course in due process covering such areas as tort, discrimination, sexual harassment, denial of benefits etc. The areas of responsibility do not include performance reviews, pay levels, change in work procedures or layoffs and job elimination.

The review is done when the normal course of conflict resolution has failed. Employees must file in a complaint within an agreed time. Management decides whether the request for a peer review is warranted, and if so the panel of peers must meet within an established time-frame, say fourteen days to review the case and render a verdict within a 30 day period. Hearings usually take place on the working premises, and are conducted by a three to five members panel. If both the employee and the employer are satisfied with the panel's verdict an agreement is signed. If no agreement is reached, there can exists a further appeal to another panel before an outside mediator is sought.

Those companies such as, River Steel Co. in New Jersey or Darden Industries Inc. who have used such a method to resolve conflict, have found it very successful. There is however some word of caution, because peer reviews may not work in a unionized environment, where the culture can cause a significant barrier. On the other hand, it could certainly work in a white-collar environment where collective bargaining agreements do not usually exist

Active Listening

One of the fundamental principles of conflict resolution is that all parties should work together to reach a satisfactory conclusion. To create good communication we should start with active listening. If we do not listen, the likelihood of understanding the other party is minimal, and it certainly will not lead to a proper response.

The use of active listening starts with basic acknowledgments, such as, nodding in agreement, positive body language, good eye contact and short verbal acknowledgments. This behavior is necessary to indicate to the other party that you are actively listening and sending a positive message. Asking questions is a means of gathering information and letting the other party know that you are listening and are interested in what is being said. Sometimes silence may be golden, and it may be used to gather more information and/or give the other party an opportunity to respond. Silence is often more commonly used in the oriental culture and seems to work very effectively during difficult negotiations.

In dealing with conflict, emotions often enter into the equation. Very often, emotions are the cause of breakdowns in conflict resolution and they can create responses, which can be viewed, as accusatory and non-emphatic. In addition to the steps mentioned above, two supplementary steps can be used to remove the emotional factor from the discussions. The first one is the use of paraphrasing to summarize, clarify, and reinforce understanding of the other party's statements. It is a verification method that also indicates that one is focused on the content and the issue put forward by the other party.

Reflective listening, on the other hand, is used to respond to the speaker's emotions. This technique allows the listener to identify and respond to the speaker's emotions, which could be blurring the issues. Used in conjunction with paraphrasing it can be a very important tool in conflict resolution.

Conflict is a major contributor to stress. The winds of change are enough to bring about stress. It is not necessary to increase its levels by introducing conflict into the equation. Stress reduces productivity and, the sooner conflicts are resolved the quicker people get back to work and concentrate on what they should be doing in the first place. Conflict should not be avoided, but resolved as quickly as possible. Having said that, conflict can be avoided by good communication and through a corporate culture that promotes decision making through consensus.

Reaching Consensus

Today, the current means of effecting change is often through fighting and negotiating. More often than not, when people have something and want something additional, they attempt to acquire it at the expense of others. We have been brought up in a culture that fosters Win/Lose situations, and we cannot resolve any conflict without resorting to the old methodology. Life is not made up of zero-sum conflicts where someone must lose and someone must win. Instead we should be striving for conflict resolutions where the results are Win/Win solutions. This can be achieved through teamwork and reaching consensus.

What is consensus?

One of the major differences brought about by participative management, is that decision making is no longer a one person activity, but has been replaced by collective and team decision making. As we have seen above, as soon as we get two or more people involved, the possibility of conflict arises and makes agreement more difficult to reach. However, research also supports the fact that the more impact a problem has on others, the more important it is to involve others in the problem-solving process. While consensus is not always the best strategy, on certain occasions it remains a highly desired objective. It should be used when the ultimate decision requires a high degree of support from people involved in the implementation. In flatter organizations where the use of teams is more prevalent, this happens to be a more frequent occurrence. So what is consensus?

Consensus can be defined as the point at which maximum agreement has been reached, and action can follow. Unlike the democratic process, it is not reached by voting or imposing one's opinion on others, but it is rather a process of sharing ideas, creative and open discussion, evaluation of alternatives and debate to reach the best conclusion together with other members of the group. It is not about power or control. Instead it is about leadership, which facilitates the pursuance of new ideas and visions. In addition, consensus is the encouragement of individual participation and initiative, the promotion of thinking and working together with the best minds available.

However, to reach consensus, there are a number of conditions which must be fulfilled. They are the right team blend, clarity of information, positive environment, the management of meetings, idea generation, exploration of alternatives, as well as best-fit solution and evaluation.

Team Formation

The success of a team will depend on the right blend of team members. It is important that the right people are invited, and that they are given the opportunity to decline the invitation. People who are not interested should not attend, and we must understand that only people who are willing to serve can serve well. Proper selection presumes that team members are chosen for their ability, experience and motivation. Team bonding is of great importance to achieve consensus. If members know each other, it is easier to get bonding, however there are instances when team members come from different departments, backgrounds or even different countries in multi-national teams for example. Under these circumstances, considerations, which are normally taken for, granted, have to take precedence in the first stages of team bonding. In that case, it is incumbent upon the leader to ensure that members become aware of personality characteristics that are important for the successful performance of the team. Members should be made aware of these factors, so that they can make allowances for them during team deliberations.

People have different communication styles, and sometimes how we send and receive messages may be perceived in the wrong way, thus resulting in conflict. The same can be said for decision-making styles, some people are aggressive and others more passive, some intuitive and others analytical. People also have different values pertaining to beliefs, ideas and actions. Personal value systems can very often obstruct objectivity. Last, but not least, we have the characteristic of self-concept, which determines our sense of who we are, and our destination.

How we deal with these different characteristics, will have an impact on the outcome of team decisions. Hence it is important that team members are cognizant of these characteristics right from the start, and that they can develop a sense of understanding, acceptance and mutual respect for other team members in order to create a bond among themselves. To reinforce that bond, teams must be empowered to achieve their mission and prime objective. They must be given a clear mandate, whether they are to make decisions and implement them or whether they are to make recommendations only.

Morale, and effectiveness of the team will greatly depend on a clear understanding of its purpose, and it should be fully discussed at the start of the team bonding process. In addition to proper empowerment, teams should be given the opportunity to experience a winning outcome. Nothing is more conducive to bonding than the feeling of success, of achieving and accomplishing something together, especially when members know that it could not have been done through any other format or process. When all team members understand these differences, and they understand how to work around them, members will gain mutual respect for each other. While they do not always agree, they learn to accept the differences in opinions and ideas. Ultimately, team bonding makes it is easier for the team to reach consensus.

Clarity of Information

The whole intention behind working in teams is the opportunity to share ideas, facts and information in order to maximize the benefits of the decisions made by the team. All information should be recorded, preferably on flip charts and made available to all team members as a matter of record. The facilitator should have a clear understanding of the meeting and work procedure adopted by the team, and must allow for a constant flow of information between members. He or she must exercise great interpersonal skills to allow all members to contribute to the process. While more assertive members generally contribute more actively to debates, shy members should be given equal time to express and share their views. For this information gathering procedure to work effectively, the meeting process must be interactive, and include active listening, clear verbal, and congruent non-verbal communication accompanied by constant evaluation and feedback.

Listening

In the old bureaucratic organization structures, leadership meant that those who were in power exerted their dominance and authority through talking rather than listening. They presumed that they had all the ideas and it was their duty to inform others about them. In the new collaborative environment, the rare skill of listening has become a sought after competency.

Effective listening always starts with the willingness to let the speaker know that you are listening. This can be done by looking at the speaker, and by displaying patience while he or she speaks. Too often we confuse facts with assumptions and opinions. Facts are statements, which can objectively be proven to be true through logical demonstration. One must be cautious of irrelevant facts, because although true, not all facts may be related to the problem at hand. Assumptions and opinions, on the other hand, are statements that may be true, or may be an interpretation of the speakers' point of view, but cannot be proven.

Listening effectively enables the identification of the main points, and the supporting evidence as presented by the speaker. During the course of discussions, the listener will have to intuitively evaluate and question the speaker's statements to determine acceptance or rejection. Contribution to the team will be enhanced, when members are able to listen effectively to distinguish between facts and opinions, as expressed by the speaker and when members are able to authenticate or disagree with them.

Verbal/ Nonverbal Communication

While listening should be treated as a function of your contribution to the team's activities, communication of your ideas is equally as important. Speaking in public or in front of your peers, is ranked only second to the fear of death. However this fear should not preclude you to make a valuable contribution to the team. There are a number of simple steps that will help the most timid speaker to communicate effectively. The first step is to get the listeners' attention and permission to speak.

Once permission has been granted, make sure that what you have to say is in a logical structure. List or number your statements. Use the 6 'W's to make your point – what, why, where, when, who and how. State your case clearly, use complete sentences, and support your statements by facts. Do not use jargon, ambiguous terms and slang to illustrate your point. This is increasingly relevant today in the environment of multi-disciplined teams, where not everybody comes from the same profession and has the same technical background. Ensure that your presentation is accompanied by the right nonverbal messages. Your body language should match your message. Often, much of your communication and the importance of your message will be judged by the tone of your voice, accompanying gestures and demeanor, rather than the words used to deliver the message. Good eye contact, an alert and relaxed posture with a clear and a strong voice should help in that department.

Evaluation and Feedback

The team members have to know how well they are doing and how well the project is progressing. Evaluation and feedback is necessary to enable the smooth process of participative decision-making. During the course of deliberations it is good to stop and gather some feedback from the team. It is also recommended that feedback be used at the end of a presentation to ensure that the listeners understood the message and that any problems have been clarified before moving to the next stage or next speaker.

A good method to provide feedback to somebody is to either take some action, which demonstrates understanding, or ask a question that implies understanding, or support the statement by examples, which shows understanding. While factual feedback ensures that the lines of communication are open, it is also important to let other members of the team know about any emotional feedback.

Members feel understood and more comfortable when they know that people care and understand their feelings. Positive feedback enables the team to bond and build a stronger foundation and interpersonal relationships between team members. When required, this strong relationship among members of the team will also enable negative feedback to be taken in the context for which it is intended.

The use of unbiased feedback can help the evaluation of team members' contribution. Members should evaluate each other's communication skills as a regular team activity. This exercise enables individual improvement and improves the quality of the team as a whole. The evaluation should be done in a positive manner and without arguments. Members being evaluated should listen carefully in order to know the improvements required of them to meet the needs of the team.

In this atmosphere of understanding, open communication, commitment to the immediate task at hand, the bonding and mutual self-respect of team members makes it easier to reach consensus. However, it must be reminded that for people to work well together there must exist some form of organizing, planning, parameters and procedures.

Effective Team Meetings

Every meeting should be planned to provide the greatest opportunity for the team members to focus on the task at hand. While each team will have its own procedures, we shall discuss in general terms the most common parameters, procedures and organization of meetings, which will help a team to function at maximum efficiency.

To start with, any successful team should have a sense of being, purpose and direction. Once the team members have been selected a number of steps should be put in place to bring the whole group together, they are:

1. Identify the team by a name and create a mission statement that will describe the team's primary purpose.
2. Identify the team's assignment and strategies to be employed to fulfill its mission.
3. Establish the role of each team member and assign responsibility for each function.

The following functions should be chosen – a leader/facilitator, a meeting organizer, a secretary/record keeper. While these functions are the least number necessary, other members can be assigned other function as and when required. As well, nothing precludes any member to have more than one function.

However, to maintain the participative spirit of the team, it is best to spread responsibilities among as many team members as possible.

Once the team has an identity, it is time to decide on the rules and procedures which will guide the working process. The most important rule for teamwork is how decisions are to be made. The frequency of meetings, locations, as well as record keeping should also be decided, at this stage. When all of the above steps have been established, the remaining step left to enable team meetings to function with the minimum of distraction, is the actual running of meetings.

Productive Meetings

John J. Kielty once said: "Any meeting worth holding is worth planning." To help increase the quality and productivity of meetings, we should focus on the meeting process itself.

- Each meeting should have an Agenda. It should be prepared well in advance in order to provide ample notice to the participants. The location, date, time and purpose of the meeting should be clearly stated.
- A list of participants (including guests) and their specific assignments should be included.
- The Agenda should include all items to be discussed, and all participants should be given the opportunity to contribute to the discussions, by including items of interest to the Agenda. Any presentations should be identified by name as well as provide the name of the presenter. The allocated time should also be stated.
- Proper record keeping should be undertaken. The secretary/record keeper shall have the responsibility to prepare and distribute the minutes of the meeting. It is also incumbent upon this team member to ensure that presentation items, (flip-charts, overheads, slides, etc.) are properly transcribed and filed for future reference.

It is all well and good to have all these procedures for meetings in place. However for a meeting to be completely successful, the active participation of the team members is crucial. To this end I offer some additional observations that could help to improve the quality and productivity of meetings. This time let us focus on the responsibilities of the participants.

Ground Rules

For meetings to be productive and to obtain maximum benefit from participants, it is important that the team members know what is expected of them. From time to time during the course of the project, it would be advisable for the leader to reiterate the following:

- Participants should come to meetings prepared. They should gather information and be prepared to discuss the issues at hand. An informed participant is always a better team member.
- Participants should be aware of their roles. They must understand that they were chosen for the team because of their abilities and skills to work with other members, not to represent their own point of view or any special interest.
- Participants should follow the rules of the team. The objective is to reach consensus. Every member has an equal say and agrees to accept, and support all decisions taken.
- Participants should help facilitate the process, by being positive and helping other members in understanding issues. They should endeavor to follow the agreed process.
- Participants should participate through active listening, in order to make meaningful contributions.
- Participants should be respectful towards other members of the team. They should have faith in the abilities of their colleagues and enjoy the process.

These simple tenets, if and when observed by all team members, should go a long way towards providing a great working atmosphere. Respect for others and for team rules will help the process to move along, and foster discussions that will help reaching consensus easier.

There is no doubt that decisions made by more than one person, are bound to have a greater impact on implementation. The ideas of several people working together to solve a problem is far better than the old autocratic way of doing things through a 'top-down' culture. When people take part in a decision making process, they are more likely to participate willingly in the implementation stage. Very often the front line worker has more information pertaining to his or her job that the upper echelons of the hierarchy. It makes sense that these employees should participate in the making of decisions that affect them.

In order to promote an atmosphere conducive to this participative style, there are a number of things that must exist. First it is incumbent upon management to foster a culture, which promotes participation. This culture must create an environment based on mutual respect and be devoid of conflict. To this effect we discussed conflict resolution and the steps to be used to reach consensus.

Participative management, which includes collaboration, is the foundation for the workings of future successful organizations. Team decision, on the other hand, is the corner stone of collaboration in the new structure. Management should embrace it and allow workers to bring forth their ideas and contribute towards their personal and the organization's success. Instead of the old selfish and sometimes demotivating concept of the individual, the process of making decisions as a team brings cohesion and a sense of achievement to the organization as a whole.

Tips for Success

TEAM DECISIONS

Allow every team member to have a say
Teams should choose their own leaders
Do not reject ideas off hand
Rely on consensus not on coercion and compromise
Stop using 'position power' to lead teams
Have effective and productive meetings

With the adoption of the five principles discussed in Chapters 11 to 15, we are well underway to building a new type of organization. One, which fosters, encourages and maintains trust among its employees, its customers and the community at large. However, to create such an organization requires the participation of other parties, such as governments and unions. This new collaboration is discussed in Part Three of this book.

Part Three

THE CONSTRUCTION

CHAPTER 16

The Troika

"Businesses do not act individually to affect government policy; they act 'corporately' through associations."
– G. Alfred Hess, Jr.

"The truth of the matter is that you always know the right thing to do. The hard part is doing it."
– General H. Norman Scharzkopf.

PREVIOUSLY, IN CHAPTER 4 we made reference to the relationship between governments, corporations and unions. It was said, that these three institutions were so closely related that they inevitably contributed to the economic and labor relations problems in the work environment. In our opinion this is so true that it was deemed important to discuss this issue all on its own. It is believed that organizations' internal relationship cannot be divorced from the external forces applied by government on one hand and unions on the other.

The actions and reactions of these three major players are so closely related that they can be referred to as a 'troika'. The 'troika' is a three-horse drawn Russian sleigh. When the three horses pull the sleigh, maximum efficiency is gained by all three working together. In the business world we have the three institutions working side by side, but instead of working together, they often work within an adversarial environment. When they work together they achieve wonderful things, but this occurrence is often too rare. In most cases, each institution works independently to mold policies and strategies. Sometimes if it is seen to be in their interest, two of them will get together to formulate a new agreement. When this is done the third party, who was left out of the process automatically opposes the initiative or distances itself from the implementation.

In a new competitive world, it is increasingly more relevant for these institutions to work together to help the growth of their national economy and the well-being of the society that surrounds and supports them. Much of this current malaise can be found in history.

While it is important to understand the history of labor laws in industrialized countries, it is also important to review whether existing laws provide for an atmosphere that enables good labor relations. The history of labor laws starts with the problem experienced by workers prior to the industrial revolution, when most workers were in a serfdom system. Workers had no rights and all the fruits of their labor were passed to their masters. In the early 1900's workers were no better off. Blacklisting, political influence, and employers' violent intimidation of workers persisted well into the 1920's. Over the years leading to today's labor laws different governments have made changes through legislation. Today there are laws that allow for the freedom of association, and provide for a number of initiatives, which supports the rights of workers through collective bargaining. However, there are marked contrasts between U.S. and European countries labor laws. While European countries have laws that promote a more conciliatory approach, U.S. laws still favor employers in maintaining discipline in the work place. Technological advances have increased the ability of employers to control the workforce in many occupations. At first this trend was mostly apparent among blue-collar workers, but computers have made it possible for employers to increasingly control white-collar workers as well.

Power and control of the workforce has been one of the underlying strategic elements of government, corporations and unions. So much so, that in the interest of the national economy, it is advocated that all these three institutions abandon old traditions, and start working together for a common goal. Throughout this whole book we advocated a participative environment for employees and corporations to improve their work relationships. We can see the same approach, concepts and principles advocated for corporate relationships, being applied in tripartite discussions between all members of the troika. Each one of these institutions has a role to play in society, but as we move into the future a new style of leadership based on collaboration rather than confrontation is required.

However, we must also be aware of the obstacles that lie ahead. In many instances collaboration between these three parties are hampered by old concepts. Democracy in the work place is often more rhetoric than fact. Bolman and Deal better illustrate this when they wrote:

"Managers resist democracy for fear of losing the powers and prerogatives that they currently enjoy (and believe to be essential to organizational success). Traditional union leaders sometimes see organizational democracy as a management trick: a way of getting workers to accept gimmicks instead of real gains in wages and benefits. Union resistance also stems from fear that organizational democracy might produce closer collaboration between workers and management, thus undermining the role of the union. Moreover some unions, while formally democratic, are internally as authoritarian as their corporate counterparts. Democracy in the corporation leads to questions about democracy in the union as well."

The problem is while the 'troika' argues about control of the workforce; the workers are the ones who suffer. The roles of the parties involved have to be revisited. The question remains – What role is it? Because, new problems often require new solutions, perhaps a redefinition is required. Trust and teamwork are not only reserved for the corporate and work environment, it is time that governments, corporations and unions look at employing these same concepts to work together. Control and power should no longer be the ultimate goals. We should rather be looking at ways of working together to encourage growth, social balance and prosperity.

Understanding the role of each member of the troika, as well as their existing relationship is crucial. It is important to understand why they operate the way they do, and how their decisions affect workers and indirectly society. While their past *modus operandi* may have been correct for the old economy, in today's competitive and fast moving economy there is no longer a place for antagonistic and adversarial discussions between these institutions.

Governments

In the past, the role of Government has been generally seen as one of provider of services. Rightfully so, and there was a time when the government was the best provider of certain services. This situation was due to the lack of capital funding for large and expensive infrastructures, and also for industries where national security was a main concern. Generally services such as health, law and order, education, transportation, water and sewer utilities were seen as clear government responsibility. However as time went by, more and more services were added to the list of services provided by government. Today there are so many services provided by government that the costs has escalated to unmanageable proportions. The result has been enormous pressures for additional revenues, hence high levels of taxes. While taxation has never been very popular, most people recognize that a certain amount of government revenue should be raised through taxes to pay for services. Where taxes could not be raised or were not enough, much of the services were funded through debt. Many countries saw their debt levels rise so fast that they became unmanageable. Economic strategies were implemented to finance these debts, either through monetary or fiscal policies, which created havoc for many national economies. Many governments, New Zealand, and the United Kingdom, to name but two, have undertaken changes that have seen the privatization of many government services. The successes of these governments are being adopted in many other industrialized countries. The result of the transfer of responsibilities for services from the public to the private sector has caused many problems. While some jobs were assimilated by the private sector, many others were not. The restructuring by governments saw many jobs cut by the public sector, in many cases causing an increase in unemployment.

Socials programs are the responsibility of governments. However their proliferation and costs have drastically increased over the years, resulting in an enormous financial burden on the public system. While many of these programs are necessary, the size of the bureaucracy required to administer them are out of proportion. It is also a fact that many of these programs could be provided by alternative means. Instead for political reasons, most if not all of these programs have been and are still provided through the state. Very often politicians have made promises to boost these programs in order to bolster their popularity and chances for re-election. The problem with this trend is that today the economy can no longer sustain these programs in their current formats, and it will take brave politicians to cut them down drastically. As mentioned before, Margaret Thatcher's government in Britain was successful in making theses changes, but too few other politicians have had the audacity to implement similar restructuring of the public sector. Although more recently many States government are pushing back and putting into place right to work policies.

Of course with a reduction in government involvement there is a price to pay, and unemployment is one of them. On the other hand there are also the added benefits of a better financial position and the ability to cut taxes. Those countries that have reduced their deficits and debts are benefiting from their sacrifices. The lower cost of borrowing promotes a healthier economy, which in turn hopefully results in growth. Under these circumstances the level of savings and reinvestment in capital projects can fuel a robust economy in which everyone can participate and benefit.

In order to reach this quasi state of economic nirvana, governments have an important role to play. Politicians and bureaucrats must move away from the rhetoric that government should be the provider of services. They should instead become the facilitators for the provision of services. Governments should only be involved in the regulation of certain aspects of the economy, and maintain control only in essential services. Even in this role it does not mean that governments should be the provider, but in fact they should only be the watchdog and set parameters and regulations for these services to be provided by either the private sector or volunteer groups, wherever applicable.

Government's role will now be that of setting policies and formulating strategies for the management of the economy on the macro level. While some people maintain that government should be ran like a business, I do not believe that all services can be run by the profit motive. Many services such as national security, law and order cannot be provided with the intention of making a profit; however they should be run with maximum efficiency at the lowest possible costs.

To promote efficiency and productivity in the public sector, a major restructuring of the delivery of services is required. In the first place the high levels of bureaucracy must be eliminated and give way to less red tape and control of civil servants. Empowerment of civil servants is at the root of solving the inefficiency in the public sector. It is therefore advocated that the principles of collaborative management be adopted for the public sector, so as to reap the benefits already experienced by the private sector. The point I make is not to eliminate government, but to restructure the role of government. Today, much of what is done by government can and should be done by the private sector. The large bureaucracies of the public sector are rife with inefficiencies, which are the cause of the large deficits and debt load, which endangers the economy. If government seriously wants to change its role, it will require other institutions to pick up the slack and government should make the transfer easier by voluntarily setting policies to facilitate the provision of services. In so doing the government will have to see that the role of the private sector organizations and that of the unions also changes. In this case it is important to look at the roles of the other two members of the troika.

Unions & Employee Organizations

A discussion of employee organizations or Unions, as they are commonly referred to, often results in the debating parties to lose their objectivity. However, to be able to discuss employee relations and the role of government and corporations in a participative environment, it is impossible to ignore the role of unions. In order to examine the subject of employment relationships and corporations, a pragmatic approach is recommended. The idea is to investigate the issues with an open mind in order to find common ground that can benefit all parties. These areas include the role of unions as they affect productivity, wages, policies, profitability and very often, national economies.

While there is no definitive empirical evidence to support any negative effect by unions on productivity, it is also difficult to find evidence to the contrary. However, in many instances where there is conflict between management and unions, often productivity is affected. Where management and unions have stronger ties and easier relationships, often productivity is at a higher level. In these instances union involvement has a positive effect on productivity because the higher wages bargained for, tend to allow employers to recruit better employees.

Another aspect of collective bargaining, has been the handling of grievances through a very elaborate process agreed upon by both management and unions. As a result these conditions provide workers with a means of dealing with work related grievances, instead of just quitting. Coupled with this fact, very often, it is more difficult to find a better paying position and unionized workers tend to stay in their jobs longer, thus minimizing employee turnover. As Jeffrey Pfeffer (1994) wrote:

> "Moreover, the very fact of more employee control of the work process can enhance productivity. Participation in the design of work and the allocation of tasks may not only elicit more favorable attitudes but also enhance the effectiveness of the work process that results from a better division of labor and assignment of responsibilities." [2]

While many believe that unions can have a positive effect on productivity, there is also evidence that the contrary may also be true. This is specifically true, when the issue is the increasing costs of labor.

One of the stated objectives of unions is to raise wages for their membership. It is also true that the wage gains tend to be higher for lower wageworkers, and favors young people, minorities and short tenure employees. While for instance, in the United States, the effect of union wage differentials are comparatively small or not large enough to have a serious impact on a macroeconomics level, this is not true for countries which have a larger unionized workforce – European countries for example. In these countries the effect on the economy may be quite significant. Gains by unions can also trigger salary increases for non-unionized employees in order to maintain the level of differentiation. Research has shown that the union/non-union wage gap has a direct correlation with the rate of national unemployment, and union wage differences tend to be greater during times of unemployment.

The effect of rising wages can have a direct effect on the profitability of a corporation. While it was acknowledged that employee organizations could sometimes have a positive effect on productivity, the net effect of increased labor costs on profitability is not very clear. The questions are: Can the gains in productivity overcome the costs of increased wages? Or, are the unions' wage gains too great for the benefits gained through productivity which may cause a net decrease in profits? The complexities of accounting methodologies and acceptable standards make the research on the relationship between productivity, wage gains and profitability difficult. Some studies dealing with the effect of the percentage of union workers on profitability, more specifically price-cost margin at the industry level, conclude that the presence of unions does affect profitability. This occurs more frequently in industries operating in a monopolistic environment – the public sector immediately comes to mind. Barry Hirsch of Florida State University (1997) writes:

> "Unions have considerably greater ability to organize, and to acquire and maintain wage gains and membership in less competitive economic settings. Such settings include oligopolistic industries in which entry is difficult owing to economies of scale or limited international competition, or regulated industries in which entry and rate competition is legally restricted."[3]

Other studies on the other hand conclude that:

> "Unionism has no impact on the profitability of competitive firms." [4]

In effect research seems to be inconclusive on the relationship between unionized environment and profitability. However, shareholders often take a different and strict view of this relationship – to most it has a negative impact. This view also seems to be prevalent among management who are usually entrusted with overseeing the profitability of the corporation on behalf of the shareholders. Very often these views result in resistance to unions and adversarial positioning between Unions and management.

While we have discussed the effects of unions on productivity, wages and profitability in mostly a positive way, we must not ignore some of the negative sides of a unionized environment. There have been times when the strictly adversarial stance of both management and unions has caused irreparable harm to the corporation or, in some cases, even the national economy.

Corporations are increasingly reducing costs and leveraging their competitiveness through new technology. On the other hand unions have been known to have opposed the introduction of technology, thus impacting on productivity. Wage increases are not the only bargaining factors for unions. Benefits, training and increasingly job security have become the focus of negotiations. In a very competitive world where jobs and production can be moved to areas of the world where labor costs are lower, unions are getting more aggressive in their negotiation tactics to save jobs. In the past decade, at least in North America, there has been a steady decline in unionized membership, due mainly to the loss of jobs. Union leaders are not very happy about this loss in membership, hence revenues, and personal power. In fact labor is beginning to organize itself to regain some of that lost influence. In The United States, the

AFL-CIO, was very instrumental in the Obama campaign. When the economy picks up and gets into a 'boom' phase, union leaders become very aggressive and confrontational in their negotiations to recoup the loses of the past. This often results in long negotiations and sometimes, detrimental outcomes. Labor conflicts in Canada and the United States can be used to illustrate the problem. Let us look at some examples.

Hostess Brands. Inc.

Hostess Brands Inc., of Texas the makers of the famous 'Twinkies", declared bankruptcy after a long a protracted dispute with its labor unions. After CEO Greg Rayburn was unable to reach an agreement with its second biggest union who had gone on strike, there was no way out but bankruptcy. Result, roughly 18,000 employees lost their jobs. In a recession, it is irresponsible for unions to be intransigent in their demands. Unfortunately for their members, often union leaders do not necessarily see their members' wellbeing as a priority.

Then there is the case of the Edmonton teacher, Lynden Dorval who was fired for giving 'zeroes' for an assignment that some students did not hand in. His Union did not represent him as he was terminated by the school board.

The Hostess case and other cases which have produced the same result of job losses, illustrate some of the darker side of Union negotiations and the search for power by union leaders. Very often union leaders no longer represent their membership's point of view, but rather they use their position to further their careers. Several leaders today have taken the role of political negotiators and lobbyists, and are more concerned with their personal image instead of representing their members' grievances. The following joke illustrates the point:

> A union representative opened the door of his BMW, when suddenly a car came along and hit the door, ripping it off completely. When the police arrived at the scene, the union representative complained bitterly about the damage to his precious BMW.

"Officer, look what they've done to my Beeeemer!!!" he whined

"You union reps. are so materialistic, you make me sick!!!!" retorted the officer.

"You are so worried about your stupid BMW, that you didn't even notice your left arm was ripped off!!!"

"Oh my gaaaaawd . . . ." Replied the union rep., finally noticing the bloody left shoulder where his arm once was.

"Where's my Rolex????!!!!" he exclaimed.

On a more serious side, another forgotten factor is that the cost of settlement of labor disputes may often be so high as to force the corporation to restructure to remain competitive, and often these results in downsizing. Although, ultimately most disputes are settled, some do not, and result in the closure of the plant or organization, as was the case, some years ago, for the Gainers meat packers' plant in Edmonton. In this case, management had repeatedly told the unions that it could not afford the wages the workers wanted. Faced by another strike management closed the plant, resulting in the loss of 400 jobs.

Recurring strike actions, loss of competitiveness, loss of market share, and loss of jobs have created a climate where several groups are calling for revisions and changes in existing labor laws, more specifically for a 'Right to work' concept. However the blame must not be laid entirely on unions. As the counterpart to unions, we have corporations who employ the members of unions and it is important to look at their involvement in this relationship.

Corporations

The prime objective of private enterprises or corporations has been to make a profit to provide a reasonable return on investment for the owners or shareholders. This objective is based on the *Profit Maximization Model*, we talked about in Chapter 6. In Canada, the resources used to generate profit were mostly from natural or manufactured sources. More recently, this has changed through the increased use of technology. Today, the main resource is intellectual property. This resource is either in the form of technological advances or knowledge owned by individuals or groups. This new era dominated by information, instead of natural or manufactured resources, has made employees' intellectual contribution extremely important for corporations.

While the profit motive is still a very strong element of the enterprise, other factors have started to take precedence in the formulation of corporate strategies. We now see corporations more involved in the community that supports them, and employees are now treated as human assets. To go further, some experts are even advocating the introduction of intellectual asset valuation as part of the corporate balance sheet.

Globalization has brought with it other pressures, which have impacted on the strategies of corporations. The need for lower costs and better customer service in order to compete effectively with foreign competitors has often resulted in downsizing and relocation of manufacturing operations to developing countries where wages are lower. Another aspect of this change in corporate strategy is that no longer are plans made for long run productions. Due to customization and the need to innovate more manufacturing businesses are moving towards short run strategies. This shift from long to short term runs, in effect creates an environment, where lifetime job security has disappeared.

To maintain a fair return on investment for their shareholders, many corporations have resorted to using strategies, which have caused severe damage to the social fabric. The trend in downsizing and restructuring started in the eighties and has continued well into the nineties.

Previous economic downturns had a larger impact on blue-collar workers. The events of the past decade, however has affected more white-collar workers. This significant shift has shattered the security of middle management, and the middle class has been seriously affected. With a decline in middle class income, a severe drop in purchasing power followed in the mid-nineties, resulting in a recession.

Many of the management theories used, were justified. However the choice and implementation of some of these theories were at best questionable. A good example of the misuse of new management trends is explored by Edward Kay (1996):

> "Consider the re-engineering efforts of Calgary-based TransAlta Corp., Canada's largest investor-owned electric utility. In 1992, faced with impending deregulation by the Alberta government and loss of its monopoly status, TransAlta management began searching for ways to become more competitive. To that end, it hired Business Design Associates, Inc. of Alameda, Calif., headed by Chilean engineer and philosopher Fernando Flores, a former finance minister in the government of Salvador Allende . . . .
>
> Some of the "training" that 1,500 TransAlta employees received seems merely silly, such a sophomoric daily affirmation they were supposed to read, ending with a quasi-religious 'Amen.' Workers also complained about the jargon-laden terminology they were forced to use, and something called a "mood check." Supervisors would inquire about once a day into the mood of employees, so that emotional states deemed appropriate could be monitored and changed . . .
>
> While the ostensible purpose was to help workers improve their performance and ability to communicate, many found it extremely stressful and degrading. Some left sessions in tears, while others quit because of the effects it was having on their health."

If TransAlta were an isolated case, it would not be so bad. But in recent past this attempt at behavioral change of employees' attitude has been on the rise. The scary part, is that human resources management, are too often embracing these pseudo 'management prophets, and prophecies' not to improve the situation, but rather to cover their past inability in managing a troubled workforce in the first place. The above example is not the only one reported by Kay. He accounts for another case, with similar detrimental effects.

"Kathryn Markus thought she knew what she was getting into when, in the fall of 1993, her employer SaskTel, asked her to take part in a process – re-engineering program . . . The imparting of those skills would be the job of consultants from Symmetrix Inc., of Lexington, Mass. Three months later, after enduring what she describes as social isolation, manipulation, intimidation and continual rebukes in a high-pressure atmosphere at the hands of the Symmetrix consultants, Markus withdrew from the program. Two months after that she went on disability leave. That was more than two years ago. Markus hasn't worked since and is still undergoing psychotherapy to treat what her doctor and an independent psychiatrist diagnosed as post-traumatic stress syndrome. Markus maintains that it was the participants, rather than the company, that were being changed."

The use or misuse of these management fads has created a work environment where mistrust is prevalent. Workers no longer believe in the pronouncements of their employers and cooperation is at an all time low. The legacy is a string of broken careers, and a large number of employees with destroyed or low morale.

Just because many corporations embrace Machiavellian management styles, all is not that bad. By contrasts, many corporations are changing their strategies from just a purely profit making entity to being an active participant in their community. As government grants to various programs dwindle very often corporations have taken up the slack and made major financial contributions. This is not only true for many arts and education programs, but it extends to other areas. Increasingly corporations are becoming partners with governments in the improvement or construction of certain infrastructures, in what we commonly know as. P3s.

In order to become more willing and able participants in the community, corporations are going to seek more flexibility in managing their affairs to generate larger profits, which can allow them the luxury of financial contributions. One area of contention will invariably concern employee and labor relations.

Notwithstanding the strategic pressures caused by overall change in the economy, corporations are also trying to reverse the gains made by unions over the past. Because much of these past gains affect the costs of doing business, there is a clear trend that labor laws should be revised to allow for more flexibility to respond to the rapid effects of change. By the same token corporations should not seek to completely reverse the trend to gain absolute control over the workforce. The past decade has already taken its toll on employee morale and trust.

As we saw earlier, unions have successfully gained power to the point where some union leaders, have decided to promote their own agenda over and above those of their membership. When this has occurred, union members, the customer and the employer have had to pay for these decisions. In many countries labor laws protect the right to form unions and collect membership fees through direct wage deductions. These existing laws, have provided a sizable source of funds for unions to legitimately fight their causes and raise their profile, including influencing the election of political supporters. In addition, the 'closed shop' legislation has given unions enormous power in the decisions to hire and fire employees. As a result many organizations are fighting back, in many cases supported by a small number of workers. One of the most controversial issues, which is being increasingly put forward, is the 'Right to Work' concept.

One of these organizations is the Canadian based Fraser Institute. At a May 1997, forum on the subject of *'Right to Work laws: The Global Evidence in Reducing Unemployment'* several participants put forward theories about the need for changes in labor laws to react, adapt, and make the necessary change in order to operate in a global economy.

There is increasing evidence that some existing labor laws are actually detrimental to the level of employment in industrialized countries. While the United States has come out of the early nineties recession with increased growth with relatively low inflation, Europe is still struggling to recapture its former levels of productivity and economic growth. Job creation in Europe is lagging the U.S. The main reason, according to many economists including Edward Montgomery chief economist for the U.S. labor department, is that:

> "the U.S. labor market is much more flexible than that of Europe's. There is far less government regulation in the U.S., making it easier for American companies to hire-and fire – workers."[9]

Given the results seen in New Zealand, where in 1991 major changes were made to labor laws under the *Employment Contracts Act,* it is quite clear that corporations are going to seek less government regulations in matters concerning labor relations. There is no doubt that changes to existing labor laws must be effected to suit the new business environment. Corporations must be given the flexibility to pursue strategies which will maximize their return on investment, while at the same time safeguard the interest of their stakeholders, (employees, shareholders and community), to the best of their ability.

By the same token would it not be in the interest of the other parties, government and unions, to look at new strategies to increase employment? A shift towards amending current labor regulations is bound to cause friction between the different parties. It is quite possible that the victim could and will once again be the employee.

However, we have already seen another trend. Many so-called Non Governmental Organizations are aligning themselves with unions and other group to protest the working of such organizations as the World Trade Organization and the World Bank. These groups, under the guise of protecting workers in the third world, have resorted to demonstration, which have resulted in violence in the form of riots and other protests. It is well and good to defend the rights of workers in the third world, but is it the real reason or is it in support of protectionist laws to prevent competition on a global scale? I for one am very skeptical about these groups' real intentions. They now seem to have morphed into something more cynical as seen by the "Occupy Movement".

The discussion in this Chapter has covered the role, cause and effect of decisions and strategies made by governments, corporations and unions. The past actions of these three institutions, either unilateral or collective, have not often resulted in a cooperative environment. Too many times the troika has not worked well together. Depending on circumstances, two parties may come to an agreement and leave the third one in the wilderness. Consensus, although attempted, have not very often resulted in long lasting benefits.

However, not all is negative. It has been known that the troika can work together to achieve specific goals. The unfortunate part is that it usually happens after controversial and adversarial posturing by one or all parties. Governments of different political colors have their own agenda, and are influenced by either unions or corporations, or both in their decisions. These decisions affect national policies and economic strategies, which often impact on the working conditions and the level of unemployment. Almost every time, the victim is the ordinary worker.

As the winds of change affect the way we do business. All three members of the troika must realize that the old traditional bickering and posturing is no longer a viable strategy to achieve growth and wealth. A new model is required, one where the stakeholders become shareholders. This does not mean that we should return to the old socialist values, but we should thrive to create a climate where the workers are satisfied and attain self-fulfillment. An environment where employees' ideas are not taken for granted. In the end we must recognize that shared ownership promotes and fosters productivity and innovation.

The three parties must find new ways of planning and working together for the common goal of increased competitiveness in a global economy. They must realize that there must be some give-and-take in order to create and environment, which will enable the economy to prosper with the help of a contented workforce. All three members of the troika have an important role to play in the search for collaboration, both in the workplace and on larger issues of national interest, in order to reach the common goal of . . .

CHAPTER 17

Achieving Collaboration

> "Even if you're on the right track, if you just sit there,
> you're going to get run over."
>
> – Will Rogers.

> "We must not let our past, however glorious,
> get in the way of our future."
>
> – Charles Handy.

THE EVENTS OF the past, our historical legacy, the effects of a changing economic environment, the advances in technology, resistance to change, are all important and significant factors in our lives. In order to cope with the effects of these occurrences we must anticipate, learn, and adapt. We cannot improve our future if we do not learn from the mistakes of the past. Events of the late eighties and of the nineties have been so rapid and radical; that many of us can no longer recognize the environment we work and live in.

Globalization has been a significant factor in the rapid changes, which we have experienced. Many corporations have taken drastic measures to react to these pressures, and in some cases with disastrous results. Those who adopted the right strategies are thriving. Others have not even recognized the changes happening around them. This is true for many government institutions and other large bureaucratic organizations. These same organizations often operate under a culture of power, control and fear. They truly believe that, as long as they maintain secrecy and therefore control, when the circumstances improve they will still be able to operate in the old ways. Organizations, who still practice people management under the old principles, have a big surprise coming to them. The rapidity with which the world is changing will cause these prehistoric organizations to disappear like the dinosaurs.

Tidal wave, winds of change, hurricane, storm, watershed, are all metaphors used in management language, to describe change. But what is required in **'management by meteorology'** is without a doubt, the right climate. It is increasingly incumbent upon the members of the Troika to create the right climate in order for the pains of the last two decades of the twentieth century to amount to significant gains in the next millennium. Organizations must create the right climate for their employees to work in. They must foster creativity, promote expansion and growth; allow the freedom and ability for workers to contribute to the bottom line as well as the community.

However, on the macro level, what is more important is for members of the Troika, who are responsible for economic issues on the larger scale to come together to create an economic and social climate, which encourages growth and provides the opportunity for people to contribute to society.

In this book we have looked at a model that uses the four Pillars represented by the acronym – TEAM, and the five Principles which can help foster and maintain **TRUST**. We must translate them into a working style, which is going to reverse the conflicts and the problems of the past. A new economy based on information is not only a fact, but also requires a new style of leadership. First we have to look at leadership from two different perspectives.

First, on the larger scale, leadership on national and international matters where increasingly factors in one country's economy can affect the economy of other countries. Second, we must concentrate on corporate leadership that deals with the internal relationship between management and employees, and also the external relationship with the stakeholders.

In the next millennium, leadership has to be different. It cannot be one, which still puts an individual or groups of selected individuals on the top of a pyramid of subordinates where very often, power and control are the main objectives.

When we talk of organization structures, there is a certain irony, which we very often ignore. The pyramid is an edifice, which has been used as a model for the structure of most of the past century's organizations. How easy we forget the purpose for which the ancient Egyptians built pyramids. This wonder of the ancient world was built as a burial structure for the dead leaders of ancient Egypt. Is it not amazing and ironic, how management theories of the past based on this same structure has resulted into the death of loyalty and trust in our modern corporations? Still many organizations continue to operate under this particular structure. The search for power and continued control, often prevents weak leaders from seeing the harm that the top-to-bottom relationship has and continues to cause. New structural designs must replace the old organization structures in order to maximize the use of the most valuable corporate asset – **PEOPLE.**

The next millennium's leaders do not necessarily have to be at the top of the organization structure. In a collaborative and participative organization, the leader is seen to be in the center of a huge circle, made up of smaller teams and networks. Leadership within the teams is interchangeable, based on the project and the participants' competencies. It is the type and objectives of the project that should determine the leadership role. The old tradition of appointing permanent managers or supervisors should be eliminated. The team members can and should decide who should be their leaders.

Of course an organization must have some structure, lest we desire chaos. While flexibility is the new driver for organizations, there still exists a need for some form of structure. However, unlike the multi-layered organizations of the past, the new ones should be flatter, perhaps even concentric. The ultimate goal is to have organizations with a minimum of levels between management and the customer.

With leader*shift*, the role of the new leader takes the form of facilitation and coaching, not that of supervisor or sometimes, dictator. It is the ability to get people to work harmoniously towards the accomplishment of a common goal, which becomes the essence of the leader's job. Visioning and communicating ideas in order to get the right feedback from all participants are the important competencies of the new leader.

The abolition of secrecy and confidentiality is also a function of good leadership. To gain collaboration and innovation from employees very few secrets should be kept from them. After all in this new information age, it is easy to deliver and transmit messages without fear of translation or transmission problems. There is no longer a need, for middle management or any other intermediaries to facilitate good communication. The technology of video, e-mail, fax etc., is at our disposal. There are no excuses for the facts not to be reported accurately, and on a timely basis. Security may still be a concern, but it is no longer insurmountable.

Through the accurate decimation of information, the leadership role changes drastically. Leaders are entrusted with the responsibility to establish new parameters for change to reflect the economic and social environment. They must be visionaries and have the ability to translate that vision for their followers. Most of all, they must have the competencies associated with the ability to foster collaboration and facilitate the achievement of common goals by gaining the trust of their followers. Only when leaders have taken this new mantle of facilitator, and rejected the old guise of pseudo dictator, can they work in harmony to change the current climate into a better one. The new leader must take a step away from being '**macho**' and instead become a '**maestro**'.

Macro Climate

Earlier, it was said that corporations, organizations and even countries can no longer work in a vacuum. As the effects of globalization become part of our daily lives 'no one is an island'. Solving problems has become the task of groups instead of individuals. The movement of capital and information is so wide spread that we all live in a global village. Actions of individual governments have repercussions on other governments. The economic events of late 1997 in South East Asia are a reminder of our changed interdependence.

Employment, hence people, requires economic and social decisions which affect the lives of every human being in one-way or another. People management and new relationships are the central issue of this book where the treatment of people, as valuable assets and contributors, has been a repeated theme. In order to make the ideas, concepts and principles work, a new work environment is required.

Leaders within the Troika should adopt these same concepts and principles to work together and create the right macroclimate for a better society. The first step is for the Troika to realize that the world has changed and that new problems require new solutions. In the spirit of willingness to change, it is necessary to look at the current labor laws and effect the appropriate changes to allow flexibility in the work environment. Individuals have realized that the traditional 'job-for-life' type of security is gone. However, as a society we have not made the necessary changes to adapt to this new condition. When members of the G8 countries meet, they all boast about how well their respective countries are performing, but they ignore how their pronouncements affect the global economy. Unfortunately these gatherings, like the ones in Detroit in 1994 and Lille in 1996 have only produced rhetorical suggestions.

Governments must work with corporations and unions to amend the existing labor laws. Unions must understand that some of the laws that govern their existence are no longer applicable in a global economy. While the right to associate is supported, it is no longer viable to continue with the laws relating to the collection of union dues and the compulsory membership so jealously guarded by unions. The closed shop system must be abolished. It is time for workers to be able to work where they please – without any restrictions. As jobs in certain industries disappear, workers must be allowed to change their area of specialization without any barriers created by the closed shop system. It is the ability to perform rather than the membership of a particular union that really matters. We must remove the barriers, which may impede on the mobility of workers.

In Europe there is a move towards giving employment policy a higher priority. For example, in the Netherlands it has become easier for employers to reduce their staffing levels, and to prolong temporary and flexible contracts. In Italy, the concentration is on decentralizing bureaucracy, cutting employer taxes, and encouraging temporary employment coupled within increased training and education. Canada could learn from other countries to reform its current labor legislation.

In a global economy, the requirement is for a more flexible, deregulated and more market-sensitive approach, perhaps like the one practiced by Britain and the U.S. To achieve the necessary change, unions will have to operate differently and corporations will also have to adopt strategies to help existing and future employees adapt to this more flexible environment. Governments will have to put into place new legislation, removing some of the existing union protective laws in order to reduce their aggressive and often adversarial positioning. Too often in the past we have seen union/management conflicts, which have been detrimental to all concerned.

As the industrialized world comes out of the prolonged recession of the mid-nineties, we see an increase in union activism. We should watch out for strife in the public sector, involving nurses, teachers and civil servants at all levels. In the private sector we are bound to see unions flexing their muscles in the automobile and steel industry to name only two. One, of the major obstacle to resolving this issue, is that too many governments still depend on Labor Unions' support for their reelection.

While the Conservative governments of Ontario and Alberta in Canada have made the necessary changes to create a more market responsive climate, the National Democratic Party government of British Columbia, on the other hand, attempts to strengthen labors laws which will make it more difficult for corporations to become flexible and competitive. In Great Britain, where the Labour Party was reelected in 1997, the unions have not been able to flex their muscles too much. The Blair government resisted reverting back to its hard socialist policies and economic policies have continued to result in growth.

In the United States, the relationship between unions and management seems to be improving. Partnerships and collaboration is not unheard of. In fact as the past events continue to erode the size of union memberships, union leaders are seeking collaboration with management to protect workers' jobs and wages, and provide their members with more say in how their companies are run. They are also prepared to work with management in the training field to make their members' organizations more competitive.

Aaron Bernstein (1997) reports:

"Cooperation: Unions take the Initiative

*After years of skepticism, some unions are now advocating
partnerships with management. A few Examples:*

AFL-CIO Started a center for Workplace Democracy to help unions
develop expertise to get more involved in managerial issues.
LABORERS Set up a foundation with contractors to train construction
workers in specialized skills. Market and supplies workers to union and
nonunion firms.
MACHINISTS Runs weeklong courses for plant managers and local
union leaders on high-performance work systems in its Maryland
school. Sends union consultants to plant to help set up teams to lift
productivity.
NEEDLE TRADES Formed an extensive partnership with Levi
Strauss to cut costs and keep production in the U.S.
STEELWORKERS Persuaded major steelmakers to appoint
union-designated board members, Trains union leaders in business skills
so they can sit on union/management councils. "[1]

This type of union initiative is happening in the U.S., where some people find
that labor laws are biased in favor of business. Ironically, the U.S. has a lower
unemployment rate than most European countries where labor laws are more in
favor of unions and employee organizations. No wonder that proponents of 'right
to work' laws are pushing the issue.

Unfortunately, since the election of Barrack Obama as President, his proclivity
to give Unions much of what they want has changed the business climate in the
U.S. Now there is a clear trend towards reversing the union gains.

Another area that needs to be tackled by the Troika is the extent of
government involvement in business financing. In the past many corporations
have gone drinking at the trough of government finances. All members of
the Troika have, often backed these initiatives. In many cases however, these
ventures have collapsed and resulted in enormous financial loses, at the expense
of the taxpayer. The Troika must recognize that job creation is best left to the
private sector. Government financial involvement should be restricted to the bare
minimum. One of the roles of governments is to put the right legislation into
place to promote a competitive market place where corporations can survive and
create growth for the benefit of society and their surrounding community.

The answer to these problems lies in the use of collaboration among the interested parties. Working together under an umbrella of trust could go a long way to resolving many of the contentious issues, which we face as a society. Fortunately some far-sighted governments are taking the initiative in this field. Through tax reductions or incentives some governments have helped the development of industries, resulting in job creation and sustainable economic growth.

It is also incumbent upon corporations to show some commitment to the community where they have been allowed to invest, create jobs and profit. It is not right to reap the benefits in good times and leave as soon as there is no money to be made without proper planning. This means that corporations must also take an active leadership role in creating the right climate, to gain the trust of its employees and other stakeholders.

Micro Climate

Much of the current malaise that exists in corporations is due to the total lack of trust between management and employees. Most of that mistrust stems from a series of historical events which have left many employees bruised and battered mentally as well as financially. Employees who have been downsized as well as those who have survived management's double-talk of the past decade feel abused by the system. To regain employees' and sometimes customers' trust will require a different approach.

Organizations must first drop the word 'management' from the relationship between themselves and employees. Workers are not 'managed' like resources or cattle, they are in a relationship that requires a two-way transfer of ideas and ideologies. For too long, management has been associated with control, rather than working together for a common goal. Those organizations, which do not recognize that knowledge is a scarce commodity, will lose employees to competitors. Hopefully, the principles and concepts presented in this book will help organizations to adopt a more collaborative approach in their relationship with their employees.

Recognizing employees' talents and rewarding them adequately will go a long way into improving worker/organization relationship. As Bartlett and Ghoshal (1995) point out:

> "In the emerging information age, the critical scarce resource is knowledge – composed of information, intelligence and expertise. Unlike capital, knowledge is most valuable when it is controlled and used by those on the front lines of the organization. In a fast-changing, competitive, global environment, the ability to exploit knowledge is what gives companies their competitive advantage."[2]

While I agree with the substance of the above statement, I would caution leaders from using management techniques that would continue to 'exploit' workers. Organizations would do well to work with their employees in a partnership to maximize the use of know-how to become more competitive. Any continuance in treating employees like chattels will not benefit organizations.

Whenever the economy recovers from a downturn or a recession, it is the responsibility of corporations to live up to their commitments and promises made to workers during hard times. In this new era, it is important that we do not revert back to the old style so immersed into the use of rhetoric as a form of management. Organizations should ensure that they do not make pronouncements that they cannot live up to. Bad, as well as good news should be transmitted in the same manner. Although bad news is not welcomed, the delivery of truth is more appreciated by all parties concerned.

The next generation of workers will be more knowledgeable and hence more mobile. To maximize their new status, workers must be willing to accept new pay structures. The old employment contracts based on job security are no longer viable. Pay for performance should be regarded as the norm rather than the exception. A pay structure, which is made up of base pay and bonuses, can help mitigate the large layoffs that were so common in the mid-nineties.

In good economic times, bonuses can provide workers with just rewards, while in bad economic times; they may receive only base pay that does not unduly burden the corporation's bottom line. Hence resulting in fewer lay offs based on bottom line results. The effect of a flexible labor cost component, can work in both the organizations' and the employees' favor.

Most of all what is required in the work environment is respect. The respect for workers abilities and willingness to contribute is essential for harmony between employers and employees. The days of control and behavioral manipulation are dead. The new requirement is freedom of expression and the lack of fear.

When workers feel that they are respected, and they can fully express themselves without fear of recriminations, the work environment will be ripe for the enhancement of creativity and collaboration in the workplace. The result will be higher productivity and increased competitiveness unleashed by the power of the most important resource of any organization – its **PEOPLE.**

CHAPTER 18

Conclusion

THE LATER PART of the 20th century has brought many advances to mankind. Unfortunately with our gains we also had many losses. One of the most significant losses has been trust. Employees no longer trust their employers, and in society at large citizens have acquired an increasing sense of cynicism about their governments. Although, events of the past decade seem to be insurmountable in certain circumstances, all is not lost. The results of past decisions can still be corrected, provided we all make a commitment to change for the better.

One of the major obstacles has been the choice of strategies to implement change. While leaders have tried to adapt to the new constraints and pressures of a changing world, they have continued to use rehashed strategies of the past to deal with new problems. The old methods of behavioral change, has not worked in this new era, simply because employees today are different, more knowledgeable and have become more independent in their thinking. Today, employees have access to more information and are better educated than their forefathers. They not only are more knowledgeable, but they also are more adept at using their resources. In fact, the new employee no longer relies on constant supervision to perform. What they require is proper guidance and the freedom to contribute to clearly defined organizational goals.

Competitiveness in the business environment has grown exponentially. Innovation in products and customer satisfaction has become the focus of most organizations. I say, most, because not all organizations, have embraced this new philosophy. The public sector, for one has been very slow in adapting to this new climate.

To be innovative, requires that the organization and its employees become more creative. In order to foster creativity, we need a new culture. A culture, which is more supportive, more open and less, controlled. The old bureaucratic organizations, based on large hierarchies and levels of management, which have been at the heart of many of the problems of the past decade, are no longer viable. The strategies and policies which accompanied these structures must also disappear to make way for a different approach to people facilitation.

Leadership in this new age is to create a vision that can be embraced by all parties for the common good. Leaders will require the collaboration of more people to see their vision implemented properly. Leaders can no longer count on success, through delegation and control alone. The success of any strategy depends on the active participation of those people who will implement it and those who are affected by it. This philosophy of collaboration, not only applies to the work environment, but also increasingly affects the way politicians govern.

In an era dominated by the proliferation of information, the more informed masses demand that they are consulted. Informed individuals demand that their opinions are heard. Ideas flow from all directions in this new environment. To make use of this willingness to contribute, corporate as well as political leaders should embrace grass roots participation. In the past, the pyramid was the preferred model for organizations. In this book I provided, four pillars and five principles, which represent the four sides and the roof of a house. This structure is chosen because I believe that it is better to live, work and play in a home instead of a tomb.

To go beyond the problems, the negativism and cynicism of the past, to create a better future in a technologically advanced society, to build and maintain trust and collaboration we need a **leader*shift*** for the next millennium.

REFERENCES

Chapter 1

[1] Wright Lesley, Smye Marti *Corporate Abuse How 'lean and mean' robs people and profits* Key porter Books Limited 1996, p189.

[2] Toffler Alvin *PowerShift – Knowledge, Wealth, and Violence at the edge of the 21st century* Bantam Books 1991, p. 209

[3] Toffler Alvin *The Third Wave* William Morrow and Company, Inc. 1980 p 22.

Chapter 2

[1] Roy Phillipe 1990-91, The Quality and service revolution in the Public and Private Sectors *Optimum 21.4,* p7-13

[2] Gaebler. T, Osborne D. *Reinventing Government* Addison Wesley publishing Co. 1992

[3] Hammer. M, Champy. J *Re-engineering the Corporation: a Manifesto for Business Revolution* Harper Business 1993

[4] Nutt Paul C. Backoff Robert W 1993 Transforming public organizations with strategic management and strategic leadership *Journal of Management, Summer19.2* p299-347

[5] Willis George 1991, The 'Q' Word and Management Accounting *CMA Magazine July/Aug., 65.6 p28*

Chapter 3

[1] Deal Terrence E. Kennedy Allan. A. *Corporate Cultures* Addisson Wesley Publishing Co. 1982.

[2] Moss-Kanter Rosabeth *The Change Masters* Routledge 1992

[3] Payne Roy (1991). Taking Stock of Corporate Culture *Personnel Management – July*

Chapter 4

[1] Horton Thomas. R, Reid Peter.C. *Beyond the Trust Gap, Forging a new partnership between managers and their employees.* Richard. D. Irwin Inc. 1991 p. 1

[2] Kuczmarski Susan & Kuczmarski Thomas, *Values-Based leadership, rebuilding employee commitment, performance & productivity* Prentice Hall 1995

[3] Kouzes James. M, Posner Barry Z. *Credibility, How leaders gain and lose it. Why people demand it.* Jossey-Bass Publishers 1993. P 33.

Chapter 5

[1] Kopetz Gene(1997) Big payoffs from Layoffs, How the largest downsizers fared. *Business Week* Feb.24, p30

Chapter 6

[1] Tjosvold Dean W. and Mary M. *Leading the Team Organization How to create an enduring competitive advantage* Lexington Books 1991

[2] Tjosvold Dean and Mary M. *The Emerging Leader, Ways to a stronger team* Lexington Books 1993

[3] Wille Edgar and Hodgson Philip *Making Change Work* Mercury Books 1991 p 45

[4] Losoncy Lewis *The Motivating Leader* Prentice-Hall Inc. 1985

[5] Kouzes James. M, Posner Barry. Z. *Credibilty How leaders gain and lose it, Why People demand it.*Jossey-Bass Publishers 1993.

Chapter 7

[1] Orthmann Dr. Rosemary, AMA Research : electronic Monitoring & Surveillance *Employment Testing: Law & Policy Reporter* May 1997

[2] Bliss Michael 1994. The Right to speak out-and to be dismissed. Canadian Business, September, p107

[3] Edwards Martin 1998. "Whistleblowing" at work, *Accounting & Business* October 1998, p37

[4] Fierman Jaclyn 1995. Winning ideas from Maverick Managers, *Fortune* February 6, p70

[5] Archer Ron *On Teams* Richard D. Irwin 1996. P 23

Chapter 8

[1] Kouzes James. M, Posner Barry. Z *Credibility, How Leaders gain and lose it. Why people demand it.* Jossey-Bass publishers 1993

[2] Congor. J.A. (1989). Leadership: The art of empowering others. *Academy of Management Review* 3: p 17-24.

[3] Melohn Tom *The New Partnership. Profit by bringing out the best in your people, customers, & yourself* Oliver Wight publications, Inc. 1994

[4] Wille Edgar and Hodgson Philip *Making Change Work* Mercury Bools 1991 p 112

Chapter 9

[1] Walton Sally. J *Cultural Diversity in the Workplace* Richard D. Irwin, Inc. 1994 p21.

[2] Himelstein Linda, Anderson Forest Stephanie 1997, Breaking Through *Business Week*, February 17,1997, p.66

[3] Arthur Golda, Brighton Rachel1998, Brave New World *Open to the World,* Winter 1998/99

[4] *Ibid.* p.64

Chapter 10

[1] Sloma Richard. S. G*etting it to the Bottom Line. Management by incremental gains* The Free Press 1987.

[2] Carr Clay *The New Manager's Survival Manual, All the skills you need for success* John Wiley & Sons. Inc. 1995

[3] Sloma Richard. S. G*etting it to the Bottom Line. Management by incremental gains* The Free Press 1987. p.148

[4] Branch Shelly., The 100 best companies to work for in America *Fortune* January 11,1999, p118

[5] Schein Edgar. H., *Career Dynamics: Matching Individual and Organisational Needs.* Addison-Wesley. 1978

[6] Jackson Tony. How to hook the talent in the work pool. *Financial Post* April 16, 1997, p60

[7] Morris Betsy. Is your family wrecking your career (and vice versa). *Fortune* March 17, 1997. P 71.

Chapter 11

[1] Blanchard Ken, Carlos John P. & Randolph Alan *Empowerment takes more than a minute* Berrett-Koehler Publishers Inc. 19962

[2] Potts Mark and Behr Peter, *The Leading Edge* (NewYork: McGraw-Hill Publishing Co., 1987) p.115.

[3] Smith. Avie L, *Innovative Employee Communication new Approaches to Improving trust, Teamwork & Performance* (New Jersey: Prentice-Hall Inc., 1991) p. 19.

[4] Latouche. Marcel G. *Change in the Public Sector.* MBA Dissertation, University of Wales/ Manchester Business School, 1994.

[5] Fierman Jaclyn 1995, Winning Ideas from Maverick Mangers, *Fortune,* February 6, p 68

[6] Latouche. Marcel G. *Change in the Public Sector.* MBA Dissertation, University of Wales/ Manchester Business School, 1994.

[7] Blanchard Ken, Waghorn Terry, Ballard Jim *Mission Possible, – Becoming a World-Class Organization while there's still time.* McGraw-Hill 1997 p69.

Chapter 12

[1] Lawler. Edward.E.III, *Strategic pay, Aligning organizational strategies and pay systems.* San Francisco, Josey-Bass Inc. Publishers 1990. P 17.

[2] Lawler E.E.III, *The New Pay,* CEO Publication G84-7(55) Los Angeles: Center for Effective Organizations, University of Southern California, 1986

[3] Schuster Jay. R, Zingheim Patricia K. *The New Pay, Linking employee and organizational performance.* Lexington Books 1992. P 86.

[4] Finlay Richard. J. Governance debate just beginning, *The Globe & Mail* March 28, 1997,

Chapter 13

[1] O'Reilly Brian (1997) The Secrets of America's most Admired Coporations – New Ideas, New Products. *Fortune* Mar 03.

[2] De Bono Edward *De Bono's Tthinking Course* Petancor B.V 1982, p56

[3] Kao John *Jamming* HarperBusiness 1996

[4] Sternberg R.J. *The triarchic mind: A new theory of human intelligence* Viking 1988.

[5] Maslow Abraham A theory of human motivation, *Psychological Review,* 1943, vol 50, no.4, p370-3966 De Bono Edward. *Teaching Thinking* Billing & Sons Ltd., 1976. P 41

[6] Glassman Edward *The creativity factor: unlocking the potential of your team.* Pfeiffer & Company 1991. P 18

[7] Kao John *Jamming* HarperBusiness 1996, p4988

[8] De Bono Edward *De Bono's Thinking Course* Petancor B.V.1982. p52

[9] Blanchard Ken *Mission possible, becoming a World-Class organization while there's still time* McGraw-Hill 1997.p 178

Chapter 14

[1] Beck Arthur. C, Hillmar Ellis D. *Positive mangement Practices-Bringing out the best in organizations and people* Jossey-Bas Inc. 1986, p13.

[2] Dimancescu Dan *The Seamless Enterprise, Making Cross functional management work* Oliver Wight Publications Inc. 1992., p 198

[3] Nelson Bob, Good Lael, Hill Tom 1997 *You want ToMAYtoes,I want ToMAHtoes* Training-the Human side of Business June, p 59.

[4] Fierman Jaclyn 1995. Winning Ideas from maverick managers *Fortune* February 6, p 66

[5] Wright Lesley and Smye Marti *Corporate Abuse How 'Lean and mean' robs people and profits* Key Porter Books Limited 1996 p 8

[6] Coolidge Shelley Donald, 'Corporate Decency' Prevails at Malden Mills, *The Christian Science Monitor* March 28,1996

Chapter 15

[1] Hackett Donald, Ph.D., Martin Charles. L, Ph.D. *Facilitation Skills for Team Leaders* Crisp publications Inc. 1993

[2] Tagliere Daniel. A. *How to meet, think, and work to consensus.* Pfeiffer 7 Company 1992, p7

Chapter 16

[1] Bolman Lee. G, Deal Terrence E. *Reframing organizations. Artistry, Choice, and Leadership* Jossey-Bass Inc. Publishers 1991

[2] Pfeffer Jeffrey *Competitive Advantage through people – Unleashing the power of the work force* Harvard Business School Press 1994. P 165

[3] Hirsch Barry (1997) Unionization & Economic Performance: evidence on productivity, profits, Investment and Growth – *Right to Work Laws, A Fraser Institute Conference* May 16, p3

[4] Freeman B. Richard, Medoff L. James *What do unions Do?* Basic Books 1984. P 186

[5] Alberts Sheldon (1996) Chretien ready with a mediator *Calgary Herald* November 29, p A16

[6] Knapp Shelley (1997) Some workers set to return *Calgary Herald* June 7, p B1

[7] Kay Edward (1996) Trauma in real Life *The Globe & Mail Report on Business Magazine* November 1996, p 85

[8] *ibid* p82

[9] Miller Rich (1997), U.S. has 'paid the price' to create jobs *Financial Post* March7, p46

[10] Kasper Wolfgang (1997) Right to Work : Job creation New Zealand style – *Right to Work Laws, A Fraser Institute Conference* May 16

Chapter 17

[1] Berstein Aaron 1997 Look who's pushing productivity *Business Week* April 7, p 75

[2] Bartlett Christopher & Ghoshal Sumantra Changing the role of top management: Beyond systems to people. *Harvard Business Review* May-June 1995, Vol 73. No. 3, p142

Edwards Brothers Malloy
Thorofare, NJ USA
April 9, 2013